About the Author

CARL CARMER, editor of the famous "Rivers of America" series, is also author of *The Hudson* and numerous other best-selling books. His position in the literary world is an outstanding one. He has been president of P.E.N. and the Poetry Society of America, is honorary vice-president of the New York Folklore Society, and is a Councillor of the Society of American Historians. His work has been honored by the New York *Herald Tribune* Children's Spring Book Festival.

After receiving a B.A. degree from Hamilton College and an M.A. from Harvard, Mr. Carmer taught for twelve years at Syracuse University, the University of Rochester, Hamilton, and the University of Alabama. He then became a columnist for the New Orleans *Morning Tribune*. Later, in New York, he was an editor of *Vanity Fair* and *Theatre Arts Monthly*.

Since the publication of his best-selling book, *Stars Fell on Alabama,* in 1934, Mr. Carmer has devoted most of his time to writing. He now lives in century-old Octagon House on the banks of the Hudson River.

*The Hudson
River*

Carl Carmer

THE HUDSON
RIVER

Illustrated by Rafaello Busoni

Holt, Rinehart and Winston / New York

Library of Congress Catalog Card Number: 62–11172

91293–0612
Printed in the United States of America

To my godson,
Sam Adams McCleery

Contents

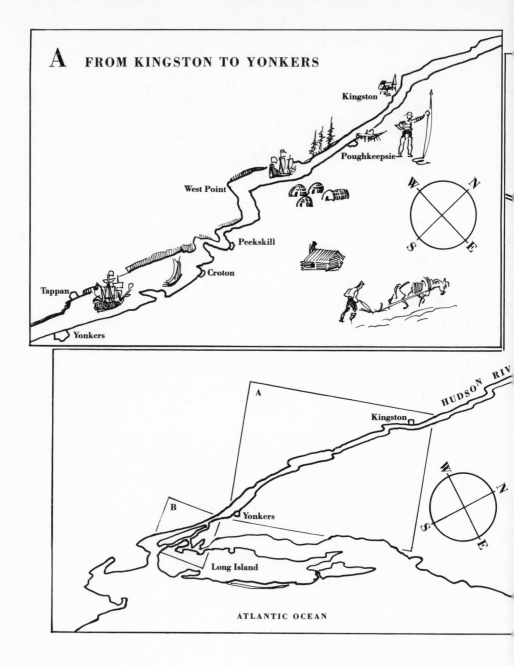

A FROM KINGSTON TO YONKERS

Kingston

Poughkeepsie

West Point

Peekskill

Croton

Tappan

Yonkers

A

Kingston

HUDSON RIV

B

Yonkers

Long Island

ATLANTIC OCEAN

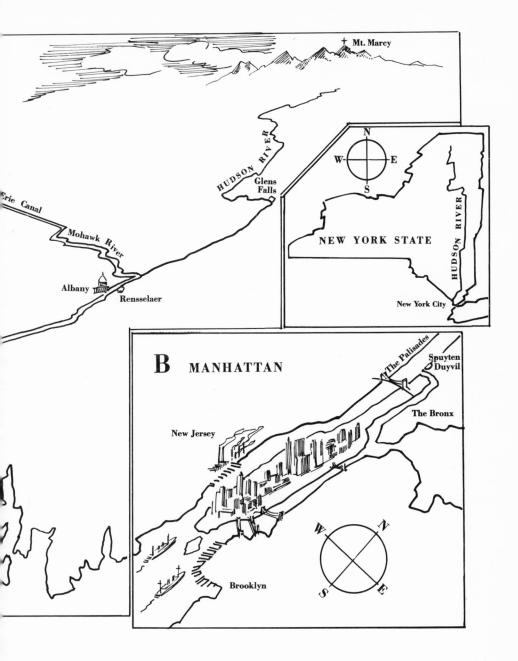

Mt. Marcy

HUDSON RIVER

Glens
Falls

Erie Canal

Mohawk River

Albany

Rensselaer

N
W E
S

NEW YORK STATE

HUDSON RIVER

New York City

B MANHATTAN

The Palisades

Spuyten
Duyvil

New Jersey

The Bronx

N
W E
S

Brooklyn

THE HUDSON RIVER

CHAPTER 1

To Make a River

Fresh waters rise from rocks as old as any in the world and flow into a little lake beside the highest peak in the Adirondack Mountains, Mount Marcy.

The Indians used to call the peak of Marcy, Tahawus, which means "the cloud splitter." The mountain called Haystack stands east of it. North of it stands Table Top; south of it stands Skylight; west of it stands Mount MacIntyre.

The little lake near the top of Mount Marcy is younger than the rocks, but it was old before men saw it. In the whole state of New York it is the highest body of water from which streams flow down toward the ocean. It was called Summit Water when Verplanck Colvin climbed to its banks in 1872. He gave it the name which it still has, "Lake Tear of the Clouds." One of the brooks which streak its sides joins others and

finally makes a big enough flow to be called a river. This is the Hudson.

Many swift streams flow into the Hudson on its way through the mountains. Below the last of these it winds east through level meadows. A few miles further on it runs into a wide, deep channel toward which it has been moving for over a hundred miles. Here it begins to flow almost straight south, and it deepens as it flows.

From the point of its southward turn, the Hudson runs over a floor that lies below the level of the sea. When the tides of the ocean rise, their waters run far up the river and meet the fresh waters from the mountains.

On its way south the river grows wider, until at one place it is

three-and-a-half miles across. There it looks like a big lake. The first Dutch people to see it called this part of the river the "Zuyder Zee." Today it is called Haverstraw Bay or Tappan Zee.

The river runs beyond the narrow island called Manhattan into New York Bay. But it has not reached the end of its channel. It cuts deep into the floor of the ocean running far to the southeast.

Thousands of years before men lived here the great stream ran through dry land to dig one of the deepest canyons the world has ever known. In some places it was 3,600 feet deep—over a thousand feet deeper than the Royal Gorge of the Colorado. If men had been in the Hudson valley then, a traveler in a boat on the river might have looked up to the blue sky between steep banks more than two miles high. Probably no man has ever seen this canyon. After the river created it, the salt sea flowed into and over it. Ever since, it has been buried deep under the tossing waves.

The naturalist-explorer William Beebe once dropped his nets far down into the Hudson channel deeps. He wrote that in the water lives a fish whose eye-pockets shine like headlights. They draw small fish close enough to be eaten. He also reports "a tiny white thread of a fish" with eyes "far out on the ends of impossibly slender stalks," and a round silver fish that keeps "all its batteries of green and violet lights turned downward while it stares . . . upward." There is also a shrimp that sends out scarlet flames, and a bronze and black "scimitar-fanged sea-dragon."

CHAPTER 2

Old Moon into Stars

WANDERERS FROM THE EASTERN TIP of the land we now call Russia crossed the Bering Straits north into Alaska and became the first Americans. They spread south along the west coast of America, then eastward. No one knows how long it took them to cross the mountains and plains of the continent, but the story of the journey was remembered by the Algonkin Indians. For a forgotten reason they set out from their homes beside the Pacific, traveling east to find the water-that-flows-two-ways.

Long years of wandering followed, but at last the Algonkins came to a wide river where they saw the downcurrent stop and an upcurrent start with the changing tide. They had found the water-that-flows-two-ways. This river would someday be called the Hudson. Eagerly they spread out along the shores in small tribes. They painted and engraved rocks and blazed trees to mark these lands as their own.

The Algonkin Indians were a simple people and good to look at. Their dusky bodies were strong and tall. White settlers found them more pleasing to the eye than to the nose. The Indians rubbed themselves with the bad-smelling grease of dead wild animals. They went about naked to the waist in warm weather. The summer clothing of a man was a breech clout, hip-length leggings of tanned hide, and soft-soled moccasins. He never owned a long feather war bonnet such as the Plains Indians wore. The River Indian usually burned most of the hair off his head with hot stones. He left a strip of stiff short hair running from the forehead to the back of the neck and, hanging from the crown, one long lock—the scalp lock that his enemies fought to take from him.

The women's leggings were knee-high. Their square leather aprons were tied about their waists and did not reach to the knees. They wore moccasins and square beaded caps, which covered the long black braids they piled on their heads. In cold weather, both men and women wore robes made from the skins of wildcat, wolf, bear, or deer, or cloaks of turkey feathers.

The River Indians colored their faces and parts of their bodies with paints made from the clay of the riverbank or from the juices of berries. The men wore shell necklaces and sometimes hung colored stones on their chests. The women covered their clothes with shell beads to make them beautiful, and to show how rich and important they were.

The Indians lived well beside the big river, which some of the tribes called the Mannahatta and others the Shatemuc. The woods were so full of birds that the noise of their twittering covered the sound of a hunter's approach. There were animals among the valley trees, too, and the Indians brought them down with arrows shot from hickory bows. They liked to eat deer, bear, and raccoon. Countless fish swam in the water. Heavy sturgeon leaped from its surface. The striped bass, the slim herring, the lavender-scaled shad swam upriver by the millions every spring. A lazy man who was also hungry could fill his stomach by picking up oysters from the river shallows.

The Indians played in the waters of the river. They swam as well as river otters. They built boats from single big trees, which they made hollow by burning and scraping. They were satisfied to stay by the water-that-flows-two-ways.

Indian villages along the Hudson looked like a number of large wooden bowls turned upside down. The builders set hickory poles into the ground. Then they bent them over until the ends met, and tied them together. They placed walls of tree bark over this frame. Inside the house the Indians dug deep fireplaces in the ground. A hole in the center of the roof let out the smoke. Long poles were dropped from the roof on strong cords made of vines. Drying corn, food baskets, and clothes were hung on the poles. Around the inside wall ran a curving bench, on which the Indians sat and also slept.

In their clearings beside the river the women of the tribes farmed the fields. They tended the yellow pumpkins that lay between the tall green corn plants. They hoed the beans. They watched over the playing children while their husbands fished and hunted. At night they ate roasted meats and loaves of corn bread. Then they sat outside their houses and watched the stars as their fathers before them had done. They measured the time of their plantings by the changing positions of the stars. They could tell what time to harvest their crops by the autumn moons.

The Hudson River Indians were not good fighters. They wished they were whenever the Mohawks left the rich valley that was named for them and came down the river in war parties. The Algonkin tribes almost always just gave the Mohawks what they wanted. The sight of a single Mohawk in war dress scared the wits out of them.

The highest chief among the Algonkin tribes was called the sachem. He thought only of peaceful living. An old record says that the sachem was looked upon as a great tree under whose shade all the tribe might rest. The sachem was to give his leadership over to the tribe's battle leader, only in time of war. It is not surprising that Henry Hudson, the first white man known to the River Indians, spoke of them as "loving people."

When there were thunderstorms, the Indians wondered how they had offended Minewawa, goddess of the valley. They asked themselves why she hurled lightning down upon them and growled at them in thunder. But they were soon dancing to thank her as the soft rains followed and made the gardens grow. The Indians burned their tobacco so that they might send clouds of smoke toward Minewawa's dwelling beyond the peaks of the Catskill Mountains in Onteora, "Land of the Sky," where they believed many gods lived. The River Indians said Minewawa hung the new moon above those peaks. It was she who took it down when it had grown old and cut it up into little stars, which she scattered about in the western sky like seeds.

One hot, hazy day the simple Indians living beside their broad river saw a strange giant moving smoothly over the water. Some of them thought it a fish sent by a faraway devil to bring evil upon them. Others saw the sun's rays on its big white wings and thought it was a bird sent by the god of light. They did not know the strange giant was a ship. They could not know that its captain was an Italian explorer.

CHAPTER 3

*"A Pleasant Land
to See"*

Giovanni da verrazano, the italian explorer, sat in the cabin of his little ship the *Dauphin* one day in July of 1524. He was writing a letter to Francis I, the King of France. The King had hired him to explore the coast of the new land of America. Da Verrazano was describing what he had seen.

"We found a pleasant place below steep little hills, and from among those hills a mighty deep-mouthed river ran into the sea . . . . We rode at anchor in a spot well guarded from the wind, and we passed into the river with . . . one small boat."

The men in the small boat sailed a short way toward the land where the river made a lake. They heard friendly shouting and saw people clothed in feathers of many colors. Some of these people jumped into a small boat and rowed toward them. Then, on a sudden ("as is wont to fall out in sailing"), the Italian sailors felt a strong gust of wind upon their faces. It forced them to go back. The *Dauphin* pulled up her anchor, spread her sails, and sailed east. Da Verrazano had come to the mouth of a river that would later be named for the English explorer, Henry Hudson, though he had not yet been born. Da Verrazano sailed away and never came back.

Eighty-five years passed before Henry Hudson saw this same river. He was captain of a small Dutch yacht called the *Half Moon*. He was sailing it along the sandy seacoast of what is now New Jersey. He had been hired by the Dutch East India Company to try to find a new route to China.

On the misty morning of September 2, 1609, the men on the *Half Moon* saw what appeared to be a great fire. It seemed to hang in the sky and no land showed beneath it. Later, the sun burned away the mists and they saw land. They sailed into a quiet bay and saw a big stream flowing into it.

The ship dropped anchor late in the afternoon. When the stars began to shine the men saw high hills to the north. They were bluer than the blue of the sky. Robert Juet, an officer of the ship, wrote in the ship's journal, "This is a very good land to fall with and a pleasant land to see."

The next day the crew pulled up the anchor and sailed north. The land was "high and bold." They sent out a boat to fish. Her men caught a big fish called a ray. It took four sailors to haul it in.

Some of the natives of the country came aboard the *Half Moon*. They wore deerskins and feather cloaks. They carried big green leaves of tobacco and brown loaves of corn bread. Beads of reddish copper hung about their necks. Their tobacco pipes were made of the same

metal. Captain Hudson went on the shore later. He wrote in his journal, "the swarthy natives all stood and sang in their fashion." He liked their country. He said, "It is as pleasant a land as one can tread upon." Robert Juet wrote that the country was full of tall oaks.

Five men were sent to sail up the river. When they came back, they said the lands they saw were covered "with grass and flowers and goodly trees as ever they had seen, and very sweet smells came from them." On the way back to the ship one of them, John Coleman, was hit in the neck by an Indian arrow and died. Darkness came and they could not see the ship. A heavy rain began to fall. All night the four men rowed about with the body of their friend in the boat. They were not able to climb back on the deck of the *Half Moon* until the next morning.

After that they were more careful. On the ninth of September two long canoes came near. The Indians in them seemed hostile. The sailors captured two of the Indians and dressed them in red coats to make fun of them.

The ship slowly sailed north on the river. They sailed by the high rock wall now called the Palisades into a very wide place like a lake. It would later be called Haverstraw Bay. The shadows of a hill ahead fell on their white sails. They turned into waters between other high hills. Robert Juet wrote, "The land grew high. The river is full of fish."

The next morning their two captives squirmed out of a round porthole and swam ashore. The Indians waited until the *Half Moon* was almost out of their sight before they shouted and laughed at her.

Fair days continued. Wildcats screamed down at them from Onteora, the Indian "Land of the Sky." The river was getting shallower. The Indians brought the white men grapes and corn, pumpkins and tobacco. They wanted to trade the skins of beaver and otter for beads, knives, and hatchets.

After fifteen days of sunny weather, a night shower rained down upon the *Half Moon*. The crew of her small boat, which had gone north in the morning, came back very wet. The men said that they had rowed until the water would not float their boat. Now Hudson knew that his hope for finding a new way to China was gone.

On September twenty-third, the *Half Moon* started sailing south. Now the autumn winds blew hard. The *Half Moon* stayed at anchor while her men explored the west bank. They said they found "good ground for Corne and other Garden herbs with great store of goodly Oakes, and Walnut trees, and Chestnut trees, Ewe trees and trees of sweet wood in great abundance, and great store of Slate for houses, and other good stones."

The reds and golds of the trees grew brighter. On the last day of the month they anchored close to the slopes where Newburgh now stands.

Early in October, some Indians boarded the *Half Moon* to trade. One of them climbed up the rudder and into an open window in the stern. There, he stole Robert Juet's pillow and two of his shirts. Then he began to climb back down to his canoe. Juet saw him and shot him dead. At once, all the natives who had come aboard jumped into the water. Some left their canoes behind and swam for the shore. The white men put out a small boat to pick up what had been stolen. An Indian swimmer tried with one hand to turn the boat over in the water. The crew's cook grabbed a sword and cut the hand off.

At last the white men were left alone. They sailed to a quiet spot beside the big island of Mannahatta at the river's mouth. There they saw a cliff "of the colour of a white greene as though it were either Copper or Silver Myne."

A northeast wind blew fiercely that night. Rain beat against the sides of the ship. Robert Juet wrote, "The fourth, was faire weather, and the wind at North North-west, we . . . came out of the River into which we had run so faire. . . . And by twelve of the clocke we were cleere of all the Inlet. Then we took in our Boat, and set our mayne-sayle and sprit-sayle and our top-sayles, and steered away East South-east, and South-east by East off into the mayne sea."

The Hudson River Indians watched the Half Moon sail out of sight. They had had their first experience with white men.

CHAPTER 4

The Hard Blond Traders

MOST OF THE FIRST SETTLERS of the valley which Henry Hudson claimed for the Dutch spoke French as their natural language. These people, called Walloons, came from homes near the seacoast of Belgium.

In April of 1624, thirty Walloon families took the ship *New Netherland*, bound for the banks of the Hudson. The Dutch company that had planned the voyage ordered them to live where they were told for at least six years. They were to plant only what they were ordered to sow. They were to be honest and respectful in their dealings with the Indians.

Soft breezes and the moon of May cast a spell upon the pioneer Walloons. A passenger, Caterina Trico, said she saw four weddings on the deck during their voyage.

Hudson's "River of the Mountains" was now called the "River of the Prince Mauritius," so named to honor a brave Dutch general.

Not all the families stayed on the river. Some went south to the Delaware River and others went east to the Connecticut River. Eight of the Walloons stayed where they landed on Manhattan Island. Their settlement was called New Amsterdam. Eighteen families sailed up the river to the foot of the long hill on which Albany now stands. There, on the west bank of the river, they set up a fort of logs and called it Fort Orange. Now there were two villages on the river.

There were also farms beside the river. But the Dutch government wanted more settlements. It was announced that thousands of acres would be granted to leaders called patroons. In return for the grant each patroon was to find many settlers who would live on his land.

A rich jeweler of Amsterdam, Kiliaen Van Rensselaer, became a patroon. He was given many acres. He set up a store in which he sold the settlers what they needed at high prices. But he would not sell any of his land to those who lived on it. He said a farmer might live on his land and plow his fields, but must pay him a share of crops and cattle each year.

The settlers did not care who ruled over them so long as they were making money. They often smuggled beaver pelts into New England where they got higher prices for them.

The traders did not even trust each other. At Fort Orange, to give everybody an equal chance to bargain, they made it a rule that no one could run up the hill to meet Indians coming in to trade. Nor could a white man let an Indian stay overnight in his house. Later, in 1664, when the English took over rule of the Hudson valley, the traders gladly gave up their loyalty to the Dutch overlords across the sea. They thought the English governors would ask a smaller share of what they had earned than the Dutch had asked.

Frontiersmen who settled New Amsterdam and Fort Orange were rough in their ideas of fun. A favorite game was Clubbing the Cat. A cat was shut up in a small barrel which hung in the middle of a tightly stretched rope. Players stood several steps away and threw clubs at the cask. The winner was the one who broke the barrel and let the cat run away.

Humor along the Hudson in Dutch days was mostly rough joking. The men galloped their horses through towns at top speed in the daytime. At night, they fired their guns and shouted.

Trader David DeVries sneaked his sloop in past Sandy Hook one dark evening. He anchored it under the walls of Fort Amsterdam. No one noticed him. At dawn, he suddenly fired three guns that made a terrific noise and "caused the people to spring out of their beds all at once."

In his very funny book, *A Knickerbocker History of New York*, Washington Irving did not show the rough-and-ready side of Dutch life. He made the Dutch seem heavy and slow. Old records of the days before English rule tell the story of a hot quarrel between Govert Loockermans, captain of the sloop *Good Hope* and a loyal subject of Holland's Prince of Orange, and Nicolas Coorn, who commanded a river fort owned by the patroon Kiliaen Van Renssalaer. Loockermans was a bold

trader, a smuggler of powder and balls to the Indians. He was sailing downriver when Coorn ordered him to lower his colors in salute with the single word: "Strike!"

"For whom?" said Loockermans.

"For the right of Rensselaerswyck," shouted Coorn.

"I'll strike for no one," said Loockermans, "except the Prince of Orange and the man I work for."

At that, Nicolas Coorn fired a cannon, and the ball whistled through the sail of the *Good Hope.*

Govert Loockermans held the staff of the flag of the Prince of Orange in his hand and shouted his answer: "Fire, you dogs; and the devil take you."

Coorn fired again, but the ball went wild. An Indian beside him then aimed his gun more surely. The bullet went through the flag of the Prince of Orange just about a foot above Govert Loockerman's head. By then the sloop had sailed too far down the river to be hit any more.

The changes Irving made in this story are interesting. He says that Govert Loockermans "of few words but great bottom, was quietly smoking his pipe." When he was ordered to lower his colors, he took his pipe out of his mouth to answer Coorn, but did not leave his chair. He did not say anything until his sloop was sailing among the Highlands many miles to the south. Then he swore so mightily that the echoes of his oaths still "give particular effect to the thunderstorms in that neighborhood." To make his story funny, Irving changed a bold, active smuggler and Indian fighter into a slow, ponderous Dutchman. Anyone who knew Govert Loockerman's history would know that the Dutch captain spoke up fiercely, and that what he said as he waved his torn flag could probably never be told by an historian.

CHAPTER 5

The English Take Control

IN THE EARLY SPRING OF 1663 the Hudson River overflowed and flooded many houses. An earthquake shook the ground. A plague of smallpox killed many settlers.

The next year brought an exciting event. Five British ships suddenly appeared. Their commander said that James, Duke of York and brother of King Charles II of England, had now become ruler of the valley.

Colonel Richard Nicolls and his British troops took control of New Amsterdam. They named the little city "New York," and went busily about explaining that England had a just claim to the colony.

The settlers were soon satisfied. The English Duke allowed them to keep their lands, and they were pleased that the taxes they had been forced to pay the Dutch West India Company were abolished.

New Amsterdam was New York; Beverwyck, the little town that had grown up about Fort Orange, was Albany; and the river of the Prince Mauritius was the Hudson. But the valley was the same. English visitors to the river found it beautiful. One of these said also "the Country itself sends forth such a fragrant smell that it may be perceived at Sea.

"The air of this provence is very good . . . generally very clear and thin . . . in the summer the Southern breezes . . . rise about 9 or 10 in the morning & continue till sunset. . . ."

A little book from Holland, *In Praise of New Netherland,* came to

the Dutch along the river. Between its covers lay a long poem written by Jacob Steendam, who had lived eight years on Manhattan.

These are four lines from it:

> This is the land, with milk and honey flowing
> With healing herbs like thistles freely growing
> The place where buds of Aaron's rod are blowing
> O, this is Eden!.

Such high praise led all newcomers to try to get land along the river shores. The English wisely allowed the Dutch patroons to hold their lands as manor lords. And if anyone could get enough land, he could become a lord.

Robert Livingston, son of a poor Scottish minister, came to the Hudson in 1674. He soon became town clerk of Albany. A few years later, according to a story told along the river for many years, he was called aboard a yacht to make the will of patroon Nicolaes Van Rensselaer. "Nicolaes the Prophet," as he sometimes called himself, was about to die, but when he saw Livingston, he had strength enough to order him away. "Anyone but you," he cried, "for you will marry my widow." Fourteen months after Nicolaes died, Robert Livingston married the widow.

Mistress Van Rensselaer had been born Alida Schuyler, and the marriage connected the young Scot with two of the richest and most powerful upriver families. Robert Livingston proved to be greedy for land. Three English governors of the colony so accused him. One of them, Benjamin Fletcher, said, "Robert Livingston never spent any money without expecting twice as much in return." The future would prove this statement to be true.

CHAPTER 6

The Tarmakers

WHILE THE SETTLERS ALONG THE Hudson were prospering, farmers in the Old World were having a difficult time. In 1707, a French army marched into the Rhine valley in Germany. It tramped down all the growing crops.

The district called the Palatinate planted new crops in the summer. But in October a north wind blew.

The valley became so cold that its precious wines froze to solid blocks of ice in their casks, and were ruined. Birds froze in flight, and fell stiff and dead to the earth. A man could not spit without the water of his mouth becoming a pebble of ice before it hit the ground. The people were starving.

In the spring a book came into the valley. The front pages were bright with gold letters. The book told the people in their own German language of a faraway river valley that was warm and peaceful. Food was to be had there for the taking. The people of the Rhine valley called this volume the "Golden Book" and read it night after night. Then Englishmen came into their country. They said their Queen Anne was kind and good. They said she owned land in warm America and would give it to people who would settle on it. They said, too, that the Queen would pay good wages to settlers who would cut down tall trees for masts on the ships of the British navy, or make tar from the contents of the pine trees.

A German preacher, Joshua Kocherthal, came to visit farms in the Palatine country. He persuaded a band of farmers to go with him to England. He said Queen Anne would send them from there to fine homes in America. There were forty-one in the group when they set out down the Rhine—ten men, ten women, and twenty-one children.

They made a happy trip down the Rhine. People met them and gave them food and clothing. Soon a boat took them free of cost to England. The Queen ordered that Kocherthal's band "should be settled upon the Hudson River in the province of New York."

In the middle of October the group sailed for New York. Their ship was nine weeks on the ocean. Their first look at the green land promised by the "Golden Book" showed them snowy cliffs and frozen rivers. These people were cared for in New York until spring. Then they sailed fifty-five miles up the Hudson and came ashore on the west bank. There, they built their homes. They called their settlement Newburgh.

While these Germans were settling at Newburgh, thousands of their countrymen were crowding into London and begging to be sent to America. It was again winter before another group sailed into the Hudson.

The Englishman, Robert Hunter, had been appointed Governor of New York. He was to go with the German settlers and to see to it that the naval stores they made would more than pay for their journey.

The six months' voyage that followed held great suffering. Twenty-eight hundred passengers on ten ships were packed into quarters too small for cattle. They lived in darkness. They lay in dirt. They breathed bad air. The ten boats sailed about near the south coast of England for four months waiting for spring and fair weather. On one of the boats, eighty people died before the end of April, The dreaded sickness called typhus caused so many deaths that it became known as "Palatine fever." When the two months of sailing across the Atlantic were over, more than four hundred had died. But there were thirty new babies to begin their lives among American woods and streams.

The arrival of almost twenty-five hundred Germans in the summer of 1710 raised the number of people living at the mouth of the Hudson by about one-half. Their first months in the new land were not the happy rich days they had expected. Only Peter Romers, coffinmaker, was making money. He sold two hundred and fifty of his boxes that summer.

When the Palatines sailed up the Hudson to their new home, the maples were a glowing red. The oaks were yellow. The pines on which they were to depend for their living were a deep green. Robert Hunter had bought them more than sixty thousand acres on the west bank of the river. He had also bought six thousand more across the river from Robert Livingston. The manor lord had got a good price for his land. He sold the new settlers things they needed at high prices.

More than eighteen hundred Germans landed on the river banks about a hundred miles upstream from Manhattan. They set up log cabins. Seven little German towns sprang up beside the river. Three of them—

Elizabeth Town, George Town, New Town—looked from the west bank across the stream toward the other four—Hunterstown, Queensbury, Annsburg, and Haysbury—on the east side, which had been bought from Livingston.

The peaks of the Catskills were white with snow when the Germans turned to the business of making naval supplies. They were to make and ship enough tar to meet the expenses of their long journey. Queen Anne had promised that when their debts had been paid, she would give every family a plot of forty acres for each of its members. All that winter the Germans planned the coming season. Richard Sackett, an English neighbor, had been hired to teach them tarmaking.

The food that had been promised the Palatine settlers by the English government became steadily worse. Jean Cast, a Frenchman who carried the supplies in his sloop to the east camp, told Governor Hunter that Livingston was cheating the settlers. Cast said, "I never saw salted meat so poor nor packed with so much salt as this pork was."

When the river ice had melted and days were warmer, the sound of axes began. The tarmakers were cutting bark from the pines and then roasting the tar from the bark. They cut the bark from a hundred thousand trees that first spring.

While their fathers swung the axes, the German boys and girls ran about the river woods. There, they picked up pine knots. By the end of the first week in June they had taken so many to the hot and smoking ovens that Mr. Sackett had been able to run off sixty barrels of tar from them. The children had gathered so many knots that Sackett was renting wagons and teams from Mr. Livingston to bring them in. Soon there were no more tar casks. Sackett was filling even the salt-pork barrels with tar.

Then, in the summer of 1711, bad luck fell upon the seven towns. Queen Anne decided to send an army against the French and their Indian allies in Canada. She ordered three hundred of the bravest and strongest German tarmakers to join her troops to help them win what was called the French and Indian war. This slowed up the making of tar.

The tarmakers were not used to working in gangs like lumberjacks. They longed to plant seeds and grow crops. They said to each other that they had come to America to find land on which their children could live "and that we cannot do here."

It would take two years before word from England's navy yards would tell them whether the results of their work were satisfactory. They had learned that the "Golden Book" and the Englishmen who had urged them to come to America had tricked them. They began to talk of a smaller valley to the northwest, the valley of the Schoharie Creek. There, a man might be free to till his own soil, and need not eat bad food or work at making tar. Whispers went around.

Governor Hunter found it harder and harder to feed these poor people. Somehow he managed to help them through the next winter and to keep them at work through the summer of 1712. At last he told them they must look out for themselves. The business of making naval stores had failed.

Some of the Germans went up and down the Hudson's banks looking for work. Others seemed too distressed to do anything for themselves. They had had faith in a new rich land. Now that land had failed them. The winter snows fell early.

Spring came and then summer. Their minister, the Reverend John Frederick Haeger, wrote back to London, "they boil grass and the chil-

dren eat the leaves of the trees. I have seen old men and women cry
that it should almost have moved a stone."

Gradually, the Palatine Germans spread out along the Hudson. Some
of them went to New York City, others to Hackensack. Some went a few
miles south of the east-bank villages to settle another little town. They
called it Rhinebeck, in memory of the German river from whose banks
they had come. One group stayed where they were on the east bank.
Their debts to Livingston grew. At last, five hundred made their way
into the valley of the Schoharie Creek.

In the years that followed, German ways and Dutch ways mixed.
Washington Irving came to visit in the river town of Kinderhook and
wandered about the country. It has been said that in his great story,
"Rip Van Winkle," the little men whom Rip found bowling among the
Catskills are very like the tiny folk that people say may sometimes be
seen in the valley of the Rhine. A family named Winkel had come to
the Hudson with the tarmakers. Perhaps it was from them that Rip got
his name. Perhaps Rip's ancestors were not Dutch, as Irving said, but
German.

The poor Palatines were only a part of a great number of people
who came early into the Hudson valley. Englishmen settled beside the
river, They planted wide fields of flax north of the city of New York.
Other settlers grew Indian corn and wheat. Hundreds of sloops brought
trade to the river ports. Rich merchants from New York City bought
country homes on the Hudson at Hoboken and at what is now Green-
wich Village. In Westchester County, by 1750, nearly five-sixths of the
people paid rent to the manor lords.

CHAPTER 7

The Story of
William and Mehitabel

Quaker hill was hard to climb in 1754. Quaker families had settled on the top of it. Few strangers dared the steep rock trail that led from Pawling to the summit. One came often though, urging his tired horse to the tall house of Jedediah Wing. He was Kilkenny Irishman William Prendergast and he came to see sixteen-year-old Mehitabel Wing. He was seldom alone with her because she was always busy taking care of her ten younger brothers and sisters. But William Prendergast had a way with him. Not many weeks had passed before he and Mehitabel were married and went down the hill together to his farm. In about a year, baby Matthew Prendergast was born.

Hard times came to William Prendergast. His crops were poor and he was behind in his rent to rich Frederick Philipse, who owned his farm. Frederick owned thousands of acres of land in Westchester County,

32

and a great manor house overlooking the Hudson at Yonkers. William found it very hard to pay a large part of his crops and his chickens to the manor lord every year.

He found out that Frederick Philipse paid the British King a yearly rent of only four pounds, twelve shillings for all his acres. That was exactly the amount William Prendergast had to pay Frederick yearly for his few acres. William felt that this was unjust. Mehitabel was soon to have a third child. He needed all the money he could get to help provide for his growing family.

Frightening news came one spring day in 1766. Two farmers had been put in jail for not paying their rent. The next morning, when William Prendergast rode out from Pawling, Mehitabel knew he would not be back by sundown. She took her children and climbed the steep trail to her father's house. There she waited for her husband, and the coming of the new baby.

In the next few days William Prendergast called for an army, and an army of farmers answered. He marched the farmers up and down their meadows. "Pay your honest debts," he said to them, "as honest men should—but not a shilling for rent."

He told his men they would march to New York the following Monday to see the Governor. Each man was to bring six days' supply of food, his gun and ammunition.

A thousand farmers came together that Monday. William Prendergast rode at their head as they moved steadily south toward New York.

Near midnight of April 20, a horseman dashed through the little city into Fort George. A few moments later, frightened citizens watched officers rush soldiers toward the fort. They knew what had happened. The terrible Prendergast and his Westchester men might enter New York

City at any time. Governor Moore offered a "Reward of One Hundred Pounds" for the arrest of William Prendergast, "the head and leader of the Rioters."

The last day of April passed slowly. Rumors were circulated that on May Day the march of the mad Prendergast and his rough men would surely reach New York. He might even order an attack in the night.

Early in the morning of May first six horsemen rode boldly up to Fort George. They had come from Prendergast to explain their actions to Governor Moore. They said their quarrel was only with the landlords. Governor Moore invited them inside the fort. He showed them a regiment of his Britannic Majesty's red-coated Grenadiers drawn up in a square. Then the six rode back to their leader. In the morning, news came that Prendergast and his farmers were headed back upriver.

Prendergast had not taken New York, but he led a victorious army. From New York to Poughkeepsie the farmers of the valley rallied to his cause. He marched on Poughkeepsie and emptied the jail of everyone who happened to be in it. Daily messengers raced for New York from the Livingstons, the Philipses, the Ten Broecks, begging Governor Moore to do something. They said that almost a thousand men were still with Prendergast. They said he was forcing decent citizens out of their homes.

By now, the rebel leader was father of a third son. The baby was named Jedediah, after the Quaker grandfather in whose house he had been born. Mehitabel and her parents were happy about the little boy. But before Jedediah was a month old, his father was in serious trouble.

From Albany, Governor Moore sent three hundred troops to restore law and order. They sailed in sloops, and landed at Poughkeepsie. When Prendergast heard that the redcoats were coming to arrest him, he marched for home.

His army consisted of only a few men when it reached the old meeting house on Quaker Hill. The men barred the doors and aimed their guns out the windows. At the Wing farmhouse, a few yards away, William Prendergast told his wife the soldiers were coming for him.

Major Browne, the British commander, set out for Quaker Hill as soon as his troops had landed. At a little wooden bridge across the Swamp River, Browne's men came face to face with thirty farmers who ran into a cornfield. Two of Browne's men were killed at the first volley from the farmers. The soldiers charged in among the tall corn stalks, but the field was still and empty. The farmers had escaped through the corn stalks.

Next morning, the British reached the meeting house. They took fifty prisoners, but not William Prendergast. The British Major was told that Mehitabel had gone to look for her husband. In a short time the twenty-eight-year-old wife in her Quaker dress and bonnet brought her husband into Browne's camp. The Major at once put Prendergast in the middle of his Grenadiers, and set them marching for Poughkeepsie as fast as their tired legs could carry them. They took their prisoner right through Poughkeepsie to a river sloop bound for New York. There, on the morning of July tenth, a crowd watched soldiers bring Prendergast ashore.

A grand jury soon charged William Prendergast with high treason. His wife was waiting at the wharf when the soldiers brought him back and marched him to the Poughkeepsie court house.

William Prendergast's trial began on August sixth. It lasted twenty-four hours. His Quaker wife was with him constantly. A reporter for the New York *Gazette* told his readers that without "the least Indecorum of Behaviour, she never failed to make every Remark that might tend to

put her husband's Conduct in the most favourable point of view."

"And when he came to make his Defence," wrote the reporter, "she stood behind him, and suggested to him everything that could be mentioned to his advantage."

The attorney general thundered that William Prendergast was the ringleader of all the rent rebels.

Mehitabel said softly that the real chief was "one Samuel Munro," who had stirred up her husband to act as he did. (She knew that Munro was safe across the Massachusetts border.)

The prosecutor called William a criminal.

Mehitabel said before the march on New York, he was "esteemed a sober, honest and industrious farmer, much beloved by his neighbors."

The angry attorney suddenly rose and said sharply to the Chief Justice, "Your Lordship, I move you that this woman be removed from the court, lest she too much influence the jury."

"She does not disturb the court," said the Chief Justice.

"Your Lordship, I do not think that she should speak at all, and I fear her very looks may too much influence the jury."

"For the same reason you might as well move the Prisoner himself be covered with a veil," snapped the Judge.

Drearily the trial came to its end. Still Mehitabel held the whole courtroom in her spell. But she could not change what had happened. The jury talked over the case.

"Guilty," said the jury foreman.

"Your verdict does not accord with the evidence," said the Chief Justice. "I must ask you to return to your deliberations."

But again the verdict was "Guilty."

The Chief Justice read the sentence, "On Friday the twenty-sixth day of September you are to be hanged by the neck until you are dead."

"God have mercy upon my soul," said William Prendergast and the reporter wrote that he said it so sadly all the people there "were melted into tears."

As the condemned man was marched to the Poughkeepsie jail, Mehitabel Prendergast was mounting her horse. She had a last chance to save her husband. She would go to see Governor Moore. She had borrowed her sister's best dress—the white one with the blue stripes—for her journey. Fort George was eighty miles away. Every moment was precious.

She galloped down the King's Road, past Fish Kill and Oscawanna Creek, past Peek's Kill, past Tarrytown. She galloped past Philipse Manor House where Frederick lived richly off the rents of poor men. Finally, she crossed the Harlem River on the slow little ferry. She dashed the length of Manhattan Island and into Fort George.

The story of Mehitabel's talk with Governor Moore is told in the Wing family to this day. She strode up and down, they say, in her pretty blue-striped linen. Her grief was so great that the Governor's eyes filled with tears. He wiped them away and said, "Your husband shall not suffer."

Then he wrote an official paper that said William Prendergast would not be hanged "until his Majesty's pleasure should be known." He let Mehitabel write in her own words a petition for the King's pardon.

As soon as she had done that, she set out for Poughkeepsie. She knew that the farmers would storm the jail and get William out, unless she could be back in time to keep them from it. If William were freed by his own men, she knew he would be relentlessly hunted down by the British authorities. She and her husband would never be able to live peaceably again.

So the ride back was more desperate even than that of the day before. By the time she galloped into Poughkeepsie, she had ridden her horse a hundred and sixty miles in less than three days.

At once she gave the Governor's order to the sheriff and rushed to tell her husband of it. At that moment the farmers had broken into the jail. They were telling William Prendergast they had come to free him. But Mehitabel would not let him go with them.

Six months later Governor Moore received a letter that said: "His Majesty has been pleased to grant William Prendergast his pardon."

So Mehitabel brought her husband back to his farm. All up and down the river, except in the big houses, there was rejoicing. The farmers had not won their battle. They would not win it for nearly a hundred years. But they were happy because William Prendergast was home with his wife and children.

CHAPTER 8

"Never to Become Slaves"

LIFE WAS HAPPIER ON THE big and prosperous farms of the rich during the eighteenth century than it was among the oppressed tenant farmers. There was something easy and graceful about life on the big Schuyler farm in the fields north of Albany. There were many slaves. The hay barn held fine saddle horses, and there was beautiful river country to ride through. There were pleasant guests and good food and good talk.

With the coming of every spring there was the day the ice broke on the river. At the first awesome cracking sound all the people of Albany ran to the shore. They did not even take off nightcaps or put on overcoats. A man who remembered these days wrote: "People never dreamed of being obeyed by their slaves until after the ice was past . . . Every child and every Negro was sure to say 'Is not this like the day of Judgment?' and what they said everyone else thought."

40

There were spring days, too, when the sky was darkened with the wings of millions of pigeons. Indians and Negroes and whites stopped what they were doing to shoot down delicious game. There were other days when the sturgeon began to swim upriver, and everybody was hard at work spearing their great bodies all day. At night hundreds of torches gave light for continuing the spearing.

Lumber rafts were on the river as soon as the melting ice raised the level of the water. The settlers put up sawmills on every stream north of Albany. After the logs had been cut, the planks were drawn to the side of the Hudson where the whole neighborhood made a large raft of them. Then the raft was floated down the river with a man or two riding on it. These men were there to steer the raft clear of islands or shallows.

Whole families sometimes rode the raft, "the mother calmly spinning, the children sporting about her, and the father fishing on one end."

The rich landowners of the valley rode and hunted, and invited each other to parties at the big houses on their vast estates. They copied the lives of those in the English country houses. And every rent day the roads to the manor houses were choked with wagons, as the tenant farmers brought in the rent they had to pay for being allowed to farm manor lands. From sunrise to sunset they waited in line to bring the manor lord a part of their crops.

By the late 1760's, people throughout the English colonies were beginning to feel anger against their rulers across the Atlantic. King George III had levied many unfair taxes upon the Americans. In the Hudson valley, manor lords, tenants, and independent farmers alike resented these taxes. Many of the colonists thought they should govern themselves.

In 1765, a mob destroyed the fine Hudson River estate of Major James of the Royal Regiment of Artillery. He had spoken too freely against people who protested the unfair taxes that the faraway British government demanded.

On April 20, 1775, a rider brought exciting news from Massachusetts Colony to Albany. The word flashed up and down the river that British soldiers had marched to seize American supplies held in Concord, and had fired upon farmers gathered to oppose them at Lexington. It was all the English-haters needed to hear. Just a month later, two hundred and twenty-five Hudson River men gathered at Coxsackie on the river to sign their names to a paper—more than a year before the Declaration of Independence was signed in Philadelphia. The paper stated that the people had made up their minds "never to become slaves."

The Coxsackie Declaration of Independence was the first to tell the world that the settlers of America would be ruled only by themselves.

CHAPTER 9

War on the River

THE PEOPLE ALONG THE HUDSON had been expecting the British soldiers. It was easy to see that if the English army could control the river, they could win the Revolutionary War. All the New England colonies would be separated from New York and New Jersey and the Southern colonies. The rebellion would be cut in two and the Continental army would easily be defeated.

When the war began, the manor lords who lived nearest to New York were on the side of the British. Those who lived on the northern manors united against them. But the leader of the upriver rebels was not one of the great landholders. He was a six-foot-four country lawyer, George Clinton, the son of a farmer in Ulster County, where men plowed their own fields and milled their own flour. He had married a Hudson River Dutch girl, and lived with his wife and two little daughters on a hill farm above the Hudson. The other farmers trusted him as leader of the defending militia because he wanted the same things they were fighting for.

In 1776, two river sloops sailed up to New Windsor, just south of Newburgh, with the news that on July twelfth, the British had landed troops at New York City. George Clinton had forty neighbors with him when he marched into Fort Montgomery on the river's west bank. He sent for more help. But the summer had brought many thundershowers, and the rain had delayed the haying. Now the farmer-soldiers were staying home to finish this task.

On the sixteenth of July, the British frigates *Rose* and *Phoenix* sailed into the Tappan Zee. A few days later they continued north. Other warships followed. One fast British sloop even stuck its nose within gunshot of Fort Montgomery.

Farmers left their horses standing among the haycocks and made for the river. Their wives rushed to the fields and drove the horses to the house doors. There, they loaded the wagons with their belongings, and rolled away to stay with relatives and friends. At points where Clinton thought British landings might be made, he placed parties of militia.

Clinton soon realized that Fort Montgomery could not be held unless it could be strengthened. He wrote to General Washington for permission to improve the fortifications and got it. An iron chain was quickly made by the valley blacksmiths, and stretched across the river from the foot of the hill called Anthony's Nose to a point below the fort.

The hated British ships had been moored above the Tappan Zee more than two weeks when five small American boats sailed after them. There was great shouting from the shore as the guns thundered. The only naval battle on the Hudson lasted for an hour and a half. By that

time the Americans knew that they could not drive the enemy away. They sailed south to Spuyten Duyvil, a little Dutch town where the Harlem River joined the Hudson, as fast as the wind would take them.

Two weeks went by, and the big boats still lay in the river. Then the Continentals thought of a daring plan. General George Washington asked Captain Silas Talbot to carry it out. Talbot's fire ship had been chased by the British warships and was anchored in a cove near them.

It was exactly two hours after midnight. Captain Talbot lay naked in his cabin. An ebb tide and a warm wind from the north were driving his craft down the river. Seaman Priestly, as naked as his commander, had set the gunpowder-filled ship adrift. Then, he helped the captain spread gunpowder trails to the fire barrels. The two men had also wet down the whole boat with inflammable spirits of turpentine. Now Priestly lay with a lighted fuse in his hand, waiting for the bump of the prow against a British ship. At that moment he would set fire to the powder trails and jump into the water. A boat would be near, with friends to row it to the shore. Just in case anything went wrong, Captain Silas Talbot held a second lighted fuse. He, too, would light a gunpowder trail and leap into the water.

For a time, Talbot could not see the ship that lay ahead. Suddenly, it was towering above him, the *Asia,* with sixty-four guns that could blast his little tinderbox into tiny pieces, if he could not drift into her. From high in the rigging of the *Asia* came a shriek—a boy's voice warning the men on deck. Hoarse shouts answered. A cannon roared. A shot splashed into the water, then another. A third hit Talbot's boat with a splintering crash. The two men on the fire ship wondered if this was to be the end of their careful plan. But they were still drifting down on the *Asia.* Priestly was now close enough to throw hooks across the rail of the *Asia.* There was a shock and a rubbing noise. The Americans dipped their fuses into gunpowder at the same time. There was a blinding flash!

When Talbot could feel and hear again, he was lying on the deck of his ship. Flames were licking at his body. He was blind. He stood up and tried to feel his way to the rail. Everything he touched was afire. He ran here and there. Then he felt the rail. A moment later he was in the water. As he swam about, he heard the voice of Priestly. Then he was lifted into a rowboat. The rowers told him three enemy ships were firing on them, as they pulled hard for the west bank. The flames of the fire ship made the river as light as day for the British gunners. The *Asia* was not yet afire, and small boats were helping her get away from the flames. Soon the fire ship was burning alone on the water.

Talbot was blistered from head to foot. He climbed out on land. He still could not see. His men quickly dragged him into the near-by woods. They led him a mile or so through thick trees. Then he heard them asking where they were. "English Settlement," said a man's voice. No, they couldn't take in anybody—not a scarecrow like that—he would frighten the town's children.

Talbot was led away. Then he heard a knock and a woman's voice. She said she was an old widow, all alone. Yes, she would care for the poor man. The men laid their captain on the floor. They covered him with a blanket and went away. They must make their report. They could not help him further.

For days and nights Talbot lay helpless and in pain. Then his sight began to come back. In a week he could see the fat body of Henry Knox, one of Washington's favorite generals, filling up the doorway of the old woman's cabin. Dr. Eustis, an army physician, came up behind the General with bandages and healing salve for Talbot's burns.

Some days later, the captain went back to General Washington's army.

While Talbot was recovering, the British ships sailed downriver. The English had had enough. They knew now that the farther up the Hudson they went, the more trouble they could expect. They knew, too, that in the valley were men who would gladly give their lives to drive them away.

CHAPTER 10

Saratoga

IN THE AUTUMN OF 1777 A strange army from Canada was marching downriver. The painted Indians were not new to the Americans, nor were the redcoats. But the Hessians with their feathered hats, their long-skirted coats, long swords, canteens the size of small barrels, their powdered hair, were strange and frightening. Though they scared some people, these hired German troops were themselves afraid of the rattle-snakes in the rocky north country. They stumbled over trees cut down to obstruct their path by the Americans. They were homesick and lonely. They tried to make up for their misery by adopting many animals as pets—black bears, deer, foxes, raccoons.

The story of the next weeks has often been told. The British claimed victory at the first battle of Saratoga, fought on the banks of the upper Hudson. But their advance was stopped for a while. They did not know that the Americans were nearly out of bullets, or they would have marched on to find little fighting ahead.

As the British rested and got ready for the next action, the Dutchmen of Albany were wildly scrambling around their roofs and windows, stripping them of lead to be made into bullets to be sent north to the American troops.

Burgoyne, the British general, was not a coward. He intended to fight. On the seventh of October he was ready. So was Horatio Gates, the American general. The Americans fought well and won.

Burgoyne began his retreat too late. The clear weather suddenly changed. A night withdrawal in a pouring rain bogged down his wagons. The British army was surrounded by the Americans at the place where Schuylerville now stands. It could not go forward and it could not retreat.

On sunny, clear October fourteenth, Major Kingston, a British officer, "well formed, ruddy, handsome," was admitted to the American camp and led blindfolded to a pleasant spot overlooking the Hudson. The young American captain, James Wilkinson, "in a plain blue frock without other military insignia than cockade and sword," was waiting for him. The British soldier spoke "with taste and eloquence on the beautiful scenery of the Hudson's river and the charms of the season." Then he took up the matter of the surrender of Burgoyne's army.

Burgoyne's British army—the Indians, the redcoats, the Hessians— had been captured by soldiers who were in clothes they wore at work in field or tavern. It was an unhealthy army, "their disease being chiefly Fever Ague and Dysentery." But it had won a great victory.

CHAPTER 11

Kingston's Burning

O N THE LOWER HUDSON, THINGS had not been going so well for the Americans. The Britisher, Sir Henry Clinton, was on the river with four thousand men. He had decided too late to go to the aid of General Burgoyne. He made a quick attack on the twin forts, Montgomery and Clinton. The American militia, led by George Clinton, fought like wildcats of the river mountains, though. British casualties were three hundred, but the redcoats took the forts at bayonet point. George Clinton saved himself by a magnificent slide down the Hudson's steep bank to the water's edge, where a boat awaited him.

The British sailed on upriver. Alarm guns boomed from the towns. Signal beacons flared from the hilltops. Still the hated white sails moved steadily north. Poughkeepsie was in a panic. Roars of big British guns echoed in the hills. Cannonballs ripped through houses as if the walls

were made of cardboard. The town of Kingston guessed what was coming. A British general had called the town "a nest of rebels . . . a nurs-
ery for almost every villain in the country." Kingston could hardly expect mercy.

At five o'clock, the white sails were off Esopus Island, just below
the town. Messengers were spurring lathered horses over country roads
to warn everybody along the river. Across the Hudson at Clermont, the
Livingstons had been working feverishly. They sent a train of wagons
filled with silver, furniture, bedding into Connecticut. In one of the
wagons sat Margaret Beekman Livingston. She laughed heartily at her
fat cook, who sat on a pile of kitchen utensils and directed her little
grandson's driving by pricking him with a long-handled toasting fork.

The Dutch folk of Kingston were not laughing. Winter was only a
month away, and the thought of a winter on the Hudson with no roof
overhead was not a happy one. Wives packed their belongings, while
husbands ran to the woods to bury things they could not take with them.
The road to Hurley, a little town three miles back from the river, was
filled with frightened people.

Three hours after the British had landed, Kingston was a smoking
ruin, and the enemy fleet was beginning its return to New York City.
Only the stone walls of the Dutch houses were left. George Clinton had
hurried to the rescue with a band of American militia. They came to the
old town just after the British had gone. They saw a burned-out town
that had not so long before been quiet and beautiful.

That winter, many of the people of Kingston built lean-tos against
the blackened stone walls of their old homes for shelter and lived in
them. Others built roofs from one wall to another. A number of them
lived with friends in near-by towns. Money and food sent by sympathetic

colonists, came up the river from as far away as South Carolina. In March, one of the first acts of a town meeting was to order many pounds of lead, which had been stored in farmer Ben Low's barn, to be made into bullets for the Continental Army. That was Kingston's answer to the British.

Another protest came from the Sterling Iron Works, thirteen miles west of the river. There, the clang of hammers on anvils was letting people know that a new chain was being forged. The rattle of iron and the jingle of harness sounded on the river road as farm wagons brought the links to New Windsor, above West Point. In April of 1778, the chain was stretched across the river from West Point to Constitution Island. Let the Britishers try to break through that!

"No king but God," shouted the people of the valley.

During the spring of 1779 the enemy began to creep up the valley once more. They took Stony Point on the west shore and Verplanck's Point opposite.

"I'll storm hell if you'll only plan it," said American General Anthony Wayne, often called "Mad Anthony" because of his reckless bravery.

"Perhaps we'd better try Stony Point first," said George Washington grimly.

Out of Fort Montgomery swung fourteen hundred men. At Springsteel's Farm near Stony Point, they halted to await the coming of evening. It was after midnight when the British sentries cried out that the Americans were below them. A half-hour later steel bayonets had done their work. The enemy's high fort had been taken. The people of the countryside were shouting in wild joy.

Thirteen—the number of states in the new nation—was the colonists' magic number. They said Wayne had taken Stony Point in just thirteen hours; that General Washington had a tomcat with thirteen rings around his tail; that the American general, Schuyler, had a topknot of thirteen stiff hairs that stood up straight on the crown of his head whenever he saw a redcoat.

CHAPTER 12

The Traitor

O<small>N A DAY OF LATE</small> September, 1780, his Majesty's ship *Vulture* sailed upriver and drifted near Teller's Point, seventeen miles below West Point. It was nearly midnight before a boat put out from the bank toward her. When it came back, a slim erect man stepped ashore. He wore an overcoat over the uniform of a British major. A figure came out from the bank to meet him. The two men talked all night, while the owner of the rowboat and his crew waited.

Morning light showed the men to be General Benedict Arnold, commander of the West Point fortifications, and Major John André, British poet, playwright, song writer. When farmer Joshua Smith refused to take André back to the *Vulture* in daylight for fear of being seen, the two officers decided to talk more at Smith's house. While they were

there, a few Americans on the east bank began to fire a small cannon at the *Vulture*. The *Vulture* sailed downriver and left its important passenger behind.

That evening, Smith, at the order of General Arnold, rowed André to the east shore. On fast horses the two officers rode the rest of the night. They ate breakfast at the home of a poor widow. Then they parted. Only a few miles lay between the Major and safety within the British lines. But three Americans who sometimes served in the Continental Army captured him near Tarrytown. They found the plans of West Point in his boots. They turned André over to Colonel Jameson, in command of Continental troops at White Plains. That officer sent a messenger to General Arnold to tell him the captured British officer had with him the plans of West Point.

Arnold was at breakfast when the message came. He read it calmly. He waited a few moments. Then he excused himself and went to tell his wife what had happened. A moment later he strolled down to the river landing and boarded his six-oared barge. He ordered the crew to row as fast as they could. He told them he was on a "mission of the greatest urgency for General Washington." But before Arnold was safe on the waiting *Vulture,* General Washington was in West Point. Arnold's traitorous plot to give West Point to the British had been discovered.

Major André was tried by a court martial. He was sentenced to be hanged as a spy. At noon on October 2nd the sentence was executed. Officers and men who would have been glad to see Benedict Arnold hanged in his place were sorry for André. Tears streamed down their faces as the gallant young British officer went to his death.

After the surrender of Cornwallis, commander in chief of the British armies, at Yorktown, Virginia, General Washington and his troops lived again on the Hudson near Newburgh. They had many months to wait before the Treaty of Paris declared the war over.

There was skating on the river, and in summer gay parties rode along the banks. Baron von Steuben, a German officer who had served as a drillmaster for the Continentals, came back from a few hours' fishing to say that he had caught a whale. His hearers discovered "whale" was his German pronunciation of the word "eel."

The autumn colors had faded in the valley on that happy November day in 1783 when General Washington left Newburgh and rode down the river road to meet Governor Clinton and General Knox with his troops at Harlem. Even as the British were sailing from Manhattan, Knox led the American army into New York.

At last the whole of the Hudson was free!

CHAPTER 13

Refugee Family

HANNAH INGRAHAM KNEW SHE WOULD never forget one of her spring days in the valley, just after the Revolutionary War had begun. It was the day her father kissed her and her younger brother, John, and told them he was going away for a while. Then he held their mother close before he set out along the road downriver. Years later Hannah told the story. Part of it went like this:

"My father lived at New Concord, twenty miles from Albany. He had a comfortable farm, plenty of cows and sheep. But when the war began and he joined the regulars they [the Rebels] took it all away, sold the things, ploughs and all, and my mother was forced to pay rent for her own farm. What father had sown they took away, but what mother raised after she paid rent they let her keep. They took away all our cows and sheep, only left her one heifer and four sheep.

"Uncle had given me a sheep, and when he found we were like to lose all, he took it away and kept it for me.

"Little John, my brother, had a pet lamb and he went to the Committee men and spoke up and said 'Won't you let me have my lamb?' He was a little fellow, four years old, so they let him have it.

"My father was in the army seven years. They took grandfather prisoner and sent him on board a prison ship.

"Mother rode fifty miles on horseback in one day when she heard it to go to see him and take him some money to buy some comforts. He had a paralytic stroke when he was there, and he never recovered, poor grandfather.

"My father was taken prisoner once but he escaped. The girl who was sent to take him his supper one night told him she would leave the door unbuttoned and he got off to the woods, but was wandering most two months before he found the army again. Mother was four years without hearing of or from father, whether he was alive or dead; any one would be hanged right up if they were caught bringing letters.

"Oh they were terrible times!

"At last there was talk of peace and a neighbor got a letter from her husband, and one inside for mother to tell her father was coming home."

Hannah's father came home on Friday, September 13, 1783. But the little family did not have much time to be happy, for he said they must leave the farm at once. He read some sentences from a newspaper in a nearby town that called men like himself "wretches, robbers, murderers." In another column he found news that a boat was waiting at the mouth of the river that would take British sympathizers away to a new country.

At once, everybody had to start getting ready. Hannah's uncle came over. The two men killed the cow and sold the beef to another farmer. A neighbor cut off the tallow and made a parcel of candles, putting in plenty of beeswax so that the tapers would be hard and good. Hannah's uncle thrashed out twenty bushels of wheat and her grandmother, who had come over with him, made bags to hold it. Hannah and John helped pack a tub of butter and another of pickles and some bags of potatoes. By Monday night, everything was ready for loading on the river sloop.

And then, on Tuesday, as they were about to set out, a crowd of angry men gathered around the house. Some of them came in and shouted fiercely and took Hannah's father away. Hannah cried all night. But in the morning her father came back. The men had decided to let him take his family out of the country.

Five wagons held all the household goods and food they took to the sloop. There were other sloops on the river and other families in them. It was a sad last journey between the river banks they all loved so well. Hannah was eleven years old when they left their home.

At the mouth of the river in New York Harbor a big boat waited. Very soon after the family had come aboard and stowed their belongings in the hold, she was on her way north. Then came weeks of stormy weather. Many of the people going to the new country were very ill, but no one died. Every few days a new baby was born and all the families aboard tried to be gay about it, but some of the older members looked sad.

The first snow of the northern winter was falling on the white tents provided for the boat's passengers by their new government in Canada, when Hannah's father led his family ashore on the bank of a bleak river.

They lived in the white tents for a few days, eating what kind strangers brought to them and saving their own bags of food. Then they rented a little boat and started up the river. It took nine days to reach the land that the government had given them. When they pitched their tent there, they had been away from their home on the Hudson just two months.

Then Hannah's father walked up the bank and through the woods until he found a fresh spring. Hannah told about it later: "He stooped down and pulled away the fallen leaves that were thick over it, and tasted it; it was very good. So there he built his home."

One morning after Hannah and John woke up in the tent by the river, they saw their father wading through the snow drifts. He told them to call their mother and follow him through the trees. He picked up a wooden chest and started out, while each one of the family picked up something useful and followed. He went so fast that they could not keep up, but they were able to track him by his footprints in the snow. Soon they heard him pounding and they saw, through the trees, the gable end of their new house.

"There was no floor laid, no window, no chimney," Hannah said, "but we had a roof at last. A good fire was blazing on the hearth and mother had a big loaf of bread with us, and she boiled a kettle of water and put a good piece of butter in a pewter bowl to eat [with] our breakfast that morning and mother said: "Thank God we are no longer in dread of having shots fired through our house. This is the sweetest meal I have tasted for many a day.' "

Hannah's father said he would finish the house in about a month. Then they could start the New Year of 1784 in a fine Nova Scotia home. They would come to love it and to forget the old farm beside the Hudson.

CHAPTER 14

Fireflies
in the Rigging

THE BIG YACHTS THAT BROUGHT the Dutch across the Atlantic were hard to sail in the narrow waters of the Hudson. Wise boatmen on the shore began planning simpler ships for river use. They finally built the Hudson River sloop. This type of boat was to become known throughout the world. It was the boat most used on the Hudson for two hundred years.

These sloops were usually about seventy feet long. Some captains ordered sloops ninety or a hundred feet long to be built.

At first sight, the Hudson River sloops seemed all mainsail. The mast was set well forward and the jib and topsail were small, while the big mainsail bellied out from the long, heavy boom.

From these sturdy ships the Dutch boatmen learned the ways of Henry Hudson's "Great River of the Mountains." They leaned on the

heavy tillers through many a windy night. They kept their eyes fixed on the points of the high horizons, where the hill slopes end and stars begin. White sails in the shadow of the Palisades moved upriver on a salty tide. Mountain waters poured down from the north to meet them. Through the wide choppy waters of Tappan Zee, the Dutch sailors kept their eyes on Hook Mountain. Its peak was always so long in view that they dubbed it "Tedious Hook." Then they scudded past Haverstraw, and through the reach known as Sailmakers to the shining curve of the Crescent. Other reaches lay above. There were Hoge's Reach, Fisher's Reach, and the sweet-smelling reach called Clover. There they could hear the wail of mountain wildcats from the shore.

Skippers found out that when it was low water at Kingston, it was high water at the Hudson's mouth. They learned to take advantage of land breezes that spring up off the Palisades and blow a little before sunrise. They had to watch for sudden squalls. When these came, they were strong enough to turn over a sloop.

The Hollander boatmen were more skillful than the English. The language of most men who "followed the river" was still Dutch even after the river came under English rule. It was not an unusual sight to see a sloop with a Negro crew and a white captain—all talking in excited Dutch. Negro slaves liked life on the river.

Dutch owners slapped vivid colors on their sloops. Prettiest of all were the Nyack sloops; trim and fancy in gold and red and green and blue stripes. Hudson River sailors have always said flat sails "just don't hold the wind." They love to see the air at work bellying the mainsail. They were wrong, as many yachtsmen of today know. But in the old days, few sights were lovelier than that of a river sloop with a bagful of wind. The gaily painted little ships looked like colored magic carpets. In a strong wind, the sails seemed about to lift them out of the water and set them flying down the river.

The packet sloops were roomy and had plenty of deck space. Passengers walked the deck during the day. Sometimes there were parties at night. Then all aboard except the busy crew would dance to the music of fiddles under the stars. Sometimes, if the dancers looked upward, they could see fireflies flashing their little lights in the rigging.

As the young republic grew and the river towns filled up, the stream was dotted with hundreds of sails day and night. Each town had its market sloops. On the way to New York City, the green of vegetables, the gold of hay and grain, the red of apples bobbed above the bright paint of the gunwales. In 1769, Albany citizens claimed more than thirty sloops. They said each one carried four or five hundred barrels of flour besides other cargo on its eleven or twelve trips a year to New York.

The captains of these sloops did errands for their whole town. They sold a farmer's harvest in the city and bought what he wished. Then they sailed back to the village to give the farmer what he had bought and the money that was left.

They matched cloth for housewives. They took care of passengers either too young or too old to care for themselves. They would stop for a pleasant chat with the captain of a passing sloop when they felt like it. They sent ashore for milk to put in their tea. They anchored so that passengers might take a walk and admire the river scenery. At the beginning of the American Revolution, they helped many a patriot family flee from the British; at the end of the Revolution, they carried weeping Tory families downriver to the big boats which would take them to a new life in Canada.

CHAPTER 15

Rolling to Hyorky
from the Catskill Shore

In the spring of 1783, the brothers Seth and Tom Jenkins from Nantucket left Providence, Rhode Island, with one hundred thousand dollars in their pockets. They wanted to find a safer place for whalers to live. Nantucket islanders had spent many a worried night in the past few years. They knew they lived too far off the New England coast to be safe from pirates or from another nation's navy. The Jenkins brothers looked at many places. Finally, they went up the Hudson as far as Claverack Landing. Here there was water for boats of any size. Here was a Dutch settlement of busy farmers who needed neighbors to trade with.

The next spring Tom Jenkins, and all the good New England salt-water folk he and his brother could persuade to come, sailed up the Hudson. They came in whale ships. They brought with them the frames of tall, new houses. They built these so close to the river that high tide sometimes floated the bowsprit of a whale ship right through a window. As soon as people from Nantucket, New Bedford, and Martha's Vineyard had landed, the men prepared to sail for the South Seas. Boats were sent downriver to fill their water casks, for Esopus Creek waters would not begin to taste bad as would most water carried on long voyages. Then the whale ships left for Hyorky—the name the whalers made up for any faraway shore. The men left behind new-built houses, a church, a school, and more whalers. They changed the name of Claverack Landing to Hudson. Soon it was a city with twenty-five whalers on the ocean.

One captain, Robert Folger, came back with a stinking cargo of sperm oil for the Jenkins' candleworks. Captain Judah Paddock came back with another. Whaler after whaler was built. The band played and cannon roared when a whale ship slid into the river. All the school children and farmers and shopkeepers cheered. They shouted "Greasy luck!" to the proud captains, who waved from the decks as they started downriver. Captain Solomon Bunker came back in the *American Hero* with the largest cargo of whale oil ever brought into the United States.

So Hudson grew. In 1797, it lost the honor of being the capital of New York State by only one vote. Albany became the capital, but Hudson kept on growing. As soon as the ice broke in the river, Hudson's ships sailed south at the rate of around fifteen a day. Tom Jenkins bought a gold-headed cane and redheaded Squire Worth had his portrait painted. When he looked at it, he scolded the painter for making him look "like a one-story house with the chimney afire."

Then in 1812 England and France began a war against each other. American ships that sailed for England might be attacked by the warships of France. American ships that sailed for France were sometimes captured by English warships. President Thomas Jefferson decided that it would be best for the nation if no American ships sailed for any foreign ports.

So tar barrels hung over the masts of the Hudson whaler ships to keep the wood from rotting. Business died out. For twenty-five years the whaling trade lay asleep.

Then, around 1830, Captain Laban Paddock and his brother, Judah, and some of the other salt-water men decided to go back to whaling. They sent out some whaling boats. These returned with hundreds of barrels of oil. The Hudson Whaling Company was started. "Greasy luck" had come back to Hudson.

This time the town did not have the river's whaling trade to itself. Both Poughkeepsie and Newburgh had smelled the rich cargo sailing by them. They decided to build ships of their own. A crowd at the dock

cheered loudly as the first Poughkeepsie whaler, *Vermont*, set sail. The whaling trade grew rapidly. During the following spring, men from Poughkeepsie and Troy built other ships and started the Dutchess Whaling Company.

The four Hudson River companies soon owned about thirty ships. Sometimes they had hard luck instead of "greasy." Captain Norton, of the *Vermont*, was stabbed to death by one of his crew. Captain Glasby of the whale ship *Meteor* out of Hudson, got tangled in the line after harpooning a whale, and was dragged overboard and drowned. But oil was still pouring into the Hudson River towns and America was paying high prices for it.

Men were needed for crews, and many an upriver farm boy signed on for a voyage to the waters off Hyorky. A Harvard College boy named Richard Henry Dana, Jr., worked his way on the brig *Pilgrim*. He wrote in his diary that the *Pilgrim's* crew had seen the Poughkeepsie whale ship, *New England*, off Patagonia and had been honored by a visit from her tall captain—Job Terry, "known in every port and by every vessel in the Pacific Ocean." While Terry told a story that lasted through his entire visit, young Dana looked over the crew that had rowed their captain to the *Pilgrim*. He said they were "a pretty raw set just out of the bush," and they "hadn't got the hayseed out of their hair." One of them "seemed to care very little about the vessel, rigging or anything else, but went around looking at our livestock and leaned over the pig sty and said he wished he was back tending his father's pigs."

Generally, the Dutch farm boys from the Hudson Valley made good sailors. The Yankees could not fool them more than once by saying, "Cast hot water and ashes to windward!" The new crews got a little nervous the first time they saw a whale, but it was not long before they could take a "Nantucket sleighride" behind a harpooned whale without fear. On lazy days they carved presents for their upriver families from the ivory of whale-bones; and shouted, "Thar she blows! Thar she white-waters!" on the busy ones. When they came home they sneered at the frosted-cake, gilt-trimmed passenger steamers that passed them on the Hudson, and laughed loudly when the rich owners of big houses on the banks held their noses as the whale smell came ashore.

Then, suddenly, the bottom dropped out of the whale trade. All prices dropped to a low level and stayed there. Some captains said the upriver businessmen were too stingy with their pay to officers and crew. The businessmen said the river towns were too far from the whale-oil markets. They said their ships were frozen in river ice for three months every winter.

The whaling captains turned traders, and their ships sailed into the Amazon, the Congo, the Orinoco, and the Plate rivers. Hudson valley people became used to ostrich feathers and elephant bone, tortoise shell and ebony, gold dust and Spanish dollars.

CHAPTER 16

The Marriage
of the Waters

EVER SINCE THE DAYS OF the American Revolution, foresighted men had been thinking of making a canal that would connect Lake Erie with the Hudson River. George Washington had discussed the idea with an Irish engineer, Christopher Colles, and Colles had talked to President Washington's friend, Gouverneur Morris, about it. Elkanah Watson, the man who thought up the American county fair, had made a journey all the way to Mount Vernon to spend an evening with Washington and suggest to him how such a project could be accomplished. All these men were agreed that if the great harvests of the West could be loaded on ships at ports on the Great Lakes and then transferred to canal boats near Buffalo at the eastern end of Lake Erie, American commerce would grow rapidly. Also, immigrants eager for fertile Western lands would crowd the canal boats on their return trips.

72

Dewitt Clinton, a nephew of General George Clinton, became Governor of New York at this time. In 1817 he saw to it that the digging of the Erie Canal, a man-made river stretching the full width of New York, was begun. The diggers began near Rome, about midway of the whole enterprise. Crews of Irish diggers at once began making a channel toward Buffalo. Other diggers, who had come from many foreign countries, extended it in the opposite direction toward Albany.

In the eight years that followed, the canal connected many of the upstate communities. Soon there was a lively trade between Rochester and Syracuse, between Utica and Little Falls. On October 26, 1825, the whole canal was finally completed. That day was marked by a big celebration.

At ten o'clock in the morning, the *Seneca Chief,* a new packet, moved from Lake Erie into the Erie Canal. At once, a battery of cannon, set along the canal for its full five hundred miles began to fire. The gunners of Rochester heard a booming in the west and pulled their lanyards. The Syracuse cannoneers sent the sound of the big guns echoing over the hills to Utica. The valley of the Mohawk carried it toward Albany. Spurts of white smoke crowned the high hills beside the Hudson, and in the Catskills, people heard sharp explosions. Man-made thunder seemed to shake the walls of the Palisades. The first message ever carried on sound waves from Buffalo to New York City had arrived in eighty-one minutes. The answer was back in Buffalo eighty minutes later. The whole state knew that the waters of Lake Erie were running through the new canal to the sea.

"Who comes there?" shouted the captain of *Young Lion of the West,* waiting at Rochester.

"Your brothers from the West on the waters of the Great Lakes."

"By what means have they been diverted so far from their natural course?"

"Through the channel of the great Erie Canal."

Then the whole valley of the Genesee River shook with cheering and the salute of guns and the bangs of fire-crackers.

The *Young Lion of the West* floated behind the *Seneca Chief.* On her deck were two wolves, a fawn, a fox, and four raccoons. On the *Noah's Ark* were two Seneca Indian boys and a black bear. Many other boats followed.

On the morning of November second, a big lock at Albany set the boats down one at a time on the waters of the Hudson.

"At ten o'clock," said the newspaper, the Albany *Advertiser,* "the *Seneca Chief* and the *Young Lion* floated free from the lock. Each was taken in tow by ten yawls, manned by a crew of four rowers."

All day the people of Albany marched through their streets in fancy uniforms. Bonfires lighted the city hilltop. There was feasting and singing along the river.

At ten on Friday morning, November third, the white steamer, *Chancellor Livingston,* led off the great ship parade. Beneath the colored streamers and fluttering banners of each vessel, a brass band played patriotic airs. Uniformed companies at Albany fired one great volley, as the fleet moved away and the people yelled and waved.

The big boats drifted downstream all day. Signal guns along the banks told the smaller towns of the passing of the "fleet from the dominion of fairies."

As darkness settled, the *Chancellor Livingston* suddenly became a great triangle of burning lanterns. Lights on other vessels were twinkling. Down by the water tar barrels burned fiercely. Rockets streaked

the sky and burst into a rain of stars. Poughkeepsie was one red glare and the thunder of many cannon.

Midnight had come when the fleet reached West Point. Twenty-four guns saluted it, as the cadet band marched aboard the *Chancellor Livingston*. Soon their music was fading into silence downriver. The night shifts went on duty, and the big steamers chugged along toward New York.

The steamboat, *Washington*, moved up from New York at sunrise to meet the long parade.

"From whence came ye?"

"An escort from Lake Erie."

"Whither bound?"

"To the Atlantic—what vessel is that?"

"The Yacht of the City of New York to welcome you into our waters."

Hundreds of bells began pealing and the city bands began to play. The Hudson was crowded with small boats. The steamer, *Fulton,* moved up beside the *Chancellor Livingston* to share with her the honor of towing out to the ocean the first canal boat ever to make the trip from the Great Lakes to New York. There were fourteen steamboats in line.

Two bright green kegs ringed with gilded hoops were brought to the deck of the *Seneca Chief.* Tall, majestic Governor DeWitt Clinton lifted one of the kegs and poured water from Lake Erie into the Atlantic.

Then America's champion speechmaker, Dr. Samuel Latham Mitchill, made a speech and emptied into the waves bottles of water sent from most of the rivers of the world.

The sailors in the harbor aboard the English sloops of war, *Kingfisher* and *Swallow,* cheered. The British bands played "Yankee Doodle," and the West Point band answered with "God Save the King."

Meanwhile, at the Battery, bugles were calling on the land parade to fall in line. The grand marshal rode first. Then came his aides. They wore white satin collars with colored rosettes and carried short, white batons tipped with gold. Sturdy woodsmen bearing axes followed on foot. After them came farmers and gardeners with spades and hoes.

The tailors marched proudly, carrying out the theme of the waters of the occasion—the wedding of the waters—with two large banners. One of these showed Adam and Eve under a tree in the Garden of Eden, with the inscription "United We Are"; and the other one said "I was

naked and ye clothed me." A little boy named Hatfield led the men of
his father's trade, the hatters. He carried a flag on which was printed:

> *Rocks and hills can't now restrain*
> *Erie's waters from the Main.*

The combmakers, as their wagon moved along, made fifty dozen
shell-and-horn combs, which they tossed to watchers. Many fire companies were in line, and the silver trumpets of the captains sparkled in
the sunlight.

That night, City Hall was lighted "by twenty-three hundred and
two brilliant lights—1,542 wax candles, 450 lamps, and 310 variegated
lamps." When the fireworks began, a gleaming willow tree, trimmed
with yellow stars, hung for a moment in the night sky, and then a pop-
lar tree lifted boughs of flame. A shower of golden rain began to fall.
The largest rockets were fired so as to fall into the Hudson. They left
behind them wide peacock tails of colored lights that drifted down into
the river. Then everybody went home.

The Erie Canal was completed. Now canal boats could bring all the
corn and wheat, the cows and pigs grown on the shores of the Great
Lakes down the Hudson to the big market of New York.

CHAPTER 17

Palaces Afloat

IN THE MID-NINETEENTH CENTURY, the streets of the river towns were a color-poster fair, as the fight for passengers began. Long blasts from tin horns called eager travelers to the landings when a steamboat was about to load. Runners claimed speed and safety for the boat they worked for, and said her rivals were slow tubs with boilers "like to blow up any minute." The runners for the new boats with copper boilers begged travelers not to risk their lives on older boats with iron boilers. The crew of the *New London* painted her boilers with copper-colored paint, and her runners shouted "copper boilers" with the loudest. One runner always told nervous old ladies his boat had "no boilers at all."

Passengers hurried to the landing at the sound of the horns. There, they might see the white steamer puffing toward them and hear the distant voice of her bell. Her little boat would be lowered. Passengers and luggage would be dumped into it. Boatmen would row it to the dock. Quickly they would unload passengers, and fill up again with travelers about to depart. The newcomers would be bumped over the water to the still-moving ship. Passengers boarded the steamer. Then the paddles would roar again. While the onlookers watched, the gilt-trimmed steamer would become a far white speck on the water.

A new passenger found himself in a crowd. Everybody talked to everybody else, and a man who raised his voice to give an opinion would soon be surrounded by a circle of eager listeners. A young English actress, Fanny Kemble, listened to her fellow passengers one day. Then she wrote: "Speechifying is a very favorite species of exhibition with the men here. The gift of gab appears to me to be more widely disseminated among Americans than any other people in the world."

The crowds jostled elbows at mealtimes in the big dining rooms. Long tables were covered with gleaming white linen. Negro waiters in white jackets rushed about. Food was hearty and well cooked. A steamboat breakfast one morning in 1829 offered English beefsteak, French fricassee, piles of American buckwheat cakes, and a dish called "Baptized Toast,"—but recognized by passengers as ordinary "milk toast."

As rivalry went on, the desire for more speed grew. Boys began to "follow the river" by learning the old place rhyme:

> *West Point and Middletown*
> *Konnosook and Doodletown*
> *Kakiak and Mamapaw*
> *Stony Point and Haverstraw*

A few years later pilots could nose a steamer up to a dock and hold her there while passengers and luggage were loaded. Price cutting be-

gan. The North River Association, largest boat-owning company on the river, was so badly defeated in its commercial rivalry with "Commodore" Vanderbilt that it offered him a large sum of money to leave the river. He took the money but did not leave.

Another owner, Daniel Drew, forced the Association to take him in. He purchased and secretly started running a rival boat under a false name. Then he persuaded his fellow directors to offer his dummy owner eight thousand dollars more than they had first said they would give for the rival boat, in order to cut out the competition. "I'll see if he'll accept," said Uncle Daniel. He took a walk around the block and came back to say that the dummy owner had accepted.

The price of a steamboat ticket from Albany to New York started at seven dollars, then dropped to two dollars in 1840. With a hundred steamboats on the river, the price went down for a while to fifty cents. Later, some boats asked no fare at all, and passengers paid only for meals and a stateroom.

Gradually, the *Olive Branch*, the *Constellation*, the *Chief Justice*

Marshall—big boats of the eighteen-thirties—gave way to the "floating palaces" of the forties. Carved figureheads stared over the river from gilded bows. On the decks, gold eagles spread their wings above gold balls resting on the tops of slim white poles.

The valley people were proud of their steamboats—"the most elegant in the world." Orchestras were introduced in 1821, and the *Chancellor Livingston* held dancing parties on its main deck. All important foreign guests were taken for steamboat rides soon after their arrival in New York.

The people felt that the big boats were the right place for public events. The "Marriage of the Waters" had proved that. But long before that ceremony, a band had played a dead march aboard the *Richmond* when at Annandale she passed the old house, Montgomery Place, on July 6, 1818. On the shore stood a lone woman who had lost her young husband, General Montgomery, in the Revolution. He had been killed at the siege of Quebec forty-three years before. Canada had placed his body in its coffin, and now the *Richmond* was carrying it to an honored burial in New York. Guns were sounding along the shore. Muffled drums were beating. After the *Richmond* had passed, Mrs. Montgomery fainted. The people of the valley sighed. They felt very sorry for her.

The *Chancellor Livingston* and five other steamers, with bands playing and banners flying, moved downriver on August 16, 1824 to give the returning hero of the Revolution, the old Marquis de Lafayette, his first sight of steamboats. In September, the *James Kent,* gleaming "like an enchanted castle upon the waters," gave him a ride after a ball given in his honor. It was two o'clock in the morning when the Marquis went aboard. A crowd of ladies in evening dress and wearing sashes which bore "a likeness of the General entwined with a chaplet of roses," rushed after him. They refused to come ashore. The *James Kent* ran aground at Tarrytown, but the ladies would not leave until they heard the brass band playing for them at West Point.

A steamboat escort was still the valley's greatest mark of favor twenty-five years later. The swift and lovely *Reindeer* proudly bore the great Swedish singer, Jenny Lind, from New York City to Albany on a summer day in 1851. Great crowds along the banks cheered the "Swedish Nightingale."

A Hudson River steamer used between fifteen and thirty cords of fat pine each trip. After Eliphalet Nott, President of Union College, found a way of using anthracite coal instead, a steamer looked less like "a horrible monster marching on the tide and lighting its path by the fire it vomited." But it still carried "fat pine" to bring up pressure for racing. Captains began tying down safety valves in order to go faster. The boilers of the *Aetna* exploded during a race and killed many passengers. So did the boilers of the *General Jackson*.

Many boats took to racing whenever one drew alongside another. In one race, a crew threw into the furnaces all the carved wooden furniture in order to increase the speed.

In a race in 1845, the *Swallow* ran into the little river island called Noah's Brig, and more than a dozen lives were lost. Again and again, newspapers complained against the captains for racing. "The passenger walks and sits and sleeps almost in contact with a volcano that in an instant may blow him to atoms," said the *Republican Telegraph* of Poughkeepsie in 1824. Yet racing continued for more than twenty-five years; until a race was the cause of the burning of the *Henry Clay* with a loss of life so horrible that public opinion called it to a halt.

CHAPTER 18

The Fatal Hudson River
Steamboat Race

THERE WAS AN EARLY HUBBUB along the Hudson at Albany on July 28, 1852. Awakened citizens in the riverside houses looked outside and saw two long, slim steamers side by side in the water. "Take the *Henry Clay!*" men shouted along the docks. Their cries were answered by others: "Be in New York first. Take the *Armenia!*" The price for the trip to New York had started at a half-dollar. But it was twenty-five cents a few minutes before departure time.

By seven o'clock, more than three hundred passengers had come aboard. The *Henry Clay* steamed out into the river. Her white-coated stewards gathered at the bow. They were waving and cheering.

The *Henry Clay* was two hundred and six feet long. She looked every inch the "new and swift steamer" she was said to be. She had cost $38,000, and she was built to beat every other steamboat on the river.

Captain John Tallman lay ill in his cabin. He knew that Mr. Thomas Collyer, proud builder and part-owner of the *Henry Clay*, would be able to command the crew for the day long trip. Collyer had recently agreed with Captain Isaac Smith, owner of the *Armenia*, that they would not race their boats. They had also agreed that the *Henry Clay* was to sail ahead of the *Armenia*.

The *Armenia* did not sail until the *Henry Clay* had left the dock, but a moment afterward she was under way. Ribbons of smoke trailed out behind the two steamers and live sparks flew from the tall smoke-stacks. The horizontal beams above the steeple engines moved up and down swiftly. The big side wheels thrashed through the water, leaving long white streaks. The *Armenia* was trying hard to catch up with her rival. The run to the town of Hudson seemed short, and the *Henry Clay* was well ahead as she swung toward the landing. There were cries of surprise as the *Armenia* failed to follow. She skipped the Hudson stop and steamed straight ahead down the middle of the river.

There were angry shouts on the Hudson dock. Passengers who had bought tickets on the *Armenia*, now steaming rapidly away without them, asked for their money back. They also objected when the price of a passage on the *Henry Clay* rose to a dollar. The landing was hurried. Baggage was thrown aboard.

The *Armenia* was over a mile ahead by the time the *Henry Clay* was again in the channel. The ladies on board and the more fearful gentlemen felt relieved. They were sure the *Henry Clay* would not try to catch up. The racing of steamers on the Hudson already had caused the loss of too many lives.

Soon the shaking of the boat, and a loud humming noise, showed plainly that the *Henry Clay* was not giving up the race. A blast of hot

air came from the boilers amidships. Some of the ladies pleaded with male passengers to ask the captain to stop the race. The gentlemen were told that the captain was ill of food poisoning in his cabin and could see no one. A lady fainted and the gentleman with her spoke to John Germaine, the chief engineer, about the danger.

"Are you afraid?" asked the officer.

"No, but the ladies are."

"The lives of my fellow officers and of the men are as valuable as those of the ladies. There is nothing to be afraid of," said Mr. Germaine.

Slowly the *Henry Clay* began to overtake the *Armenia*. The mile became a half-mile, then a quarter. When the *Armenia* swung into the landing at the town of Catskill, she was only three lengths ahead. Quickly she took on passengers and baggage. The *Henry Clay* landed before she could get away again, and the two crews shouted angrily at each other. The *Armenia* had gained three-quarters of a mile before the *Henry Clay* was once more speeding downriver. The long pursuit continued. Soot and bits of unburned coal dropped on the *Henry Clay's* decks. The shaking was more violent and the humming noise grew louder.

"If there is one gentleman aboard," said a lady loudly, "he will go and compel the captain to stop racing."

Isaac MacDaniel of Rutland, Vermont, was traveling with his wife and daughter. He tried to get to the captain to say he would throw him overboard if he did not order the racing stopped. The captain would not see him. Mr. MacDaniel then spoke to James Jessup, clerk of the boat.

Mr. Jessup said, "There is no danger here."

Now the *Henry Clay* was gaining again. She was faster in deep water. The *Armenia* seemed slow as her swift rival approached. She moved over toward the west bank as the *Henry Clay* began to come even with her. Pilot Jim Elmendorf of the *Henry Clay* nosed the boat in close to the *Armenia*. The two prows were even and only a few feet apart. The long steamers swept on like giant twins straining to the utmost, as they passed Turkey Point about five miles above Kingston. Then the *Henry Clay* shot out ahead a yard, two yards. Jim Elmendorf suddenly spun the wheel in the pilothouse and cut across the bow of the *Armenia*. There was a grinding roar as some of the *Armenia's* woodwork splintered.

The passengers rushed away from the crashing prows. Now the *Henry Clay* was pushing the *Armenia* toward the western bank. The officers of the *Armenia* had to choose between turning off her steam or being run aground. They gave quick orders, and their boat drifted clear. The *Henry Clay* steamed down the center of the channel. Her crew yelled for joy.

The *Henry Clay* had cleared Kingston before the *Armenia* landed. She pressed on at top speed in order to win by as much distance as possible. Twenty angry passengers stamped down the gangplank at Poughkeepsie. They said that they would not stay on a racing steamer. By the time the *Henry Clay* reached Newburgh, the *Armenia* was just a small white spot to the north. Ticket agents on the wharf were shouting, "Take the *Henry Clay*—the *Armenia* won't get here till night." A large number of passengers followed this advice.

The long white-covered tables in the *Henry Clay's* dining salon were crowded. People were waiting for places as the hot July afternoon began. The steamer was passing the grim walls of Sing Sing prison.

The *Henry Clay* kept up her speed. The Palisades towered above her now. She was passing the sunlit town of Yonkers. The west bank looked lonely and cool. But a rain of coal dust still dropped on the gay awnings of her top deck. Yellow sparks still darted upward in the black smoke from her stacks. The river was filled with curling white-capped waves. At three o'clock, the midday dinner was over. The journey was almost ended. A few of the passengers were laughing at a frightened man. He had gone forward on the bow and had piled his baggage up as a barricade between himself and the boilers.

No one remembered later who first saw smoke drifting from the midship hatchway. Below decks a fireman was throwing buckets of water on the burning canvas cover of the port boiler. His clothes caught fire. He staggered from the boiler room to the deck rail and jumped over.

Then the whole midship section of the *Henry Clay* burst into flames. Jim Elmendorf stood with his wife in the pilothouse. He took one look and spun the wheel over. Without slowing down, the *Henry Clay* swung sharply toward the east bank. In the smoke-filled engine room Jake Zimmerman put on full steam. He fastened the control so that the engine would work at top speed until the boat hit the shore. Then he raced to the deck. Screaming passengers began to run forward. Many on the afterdecks tried to dash through the flames toward the prow, but had to return. Helplessly, they lined the rails as the *Henry Clay* raced for the shore.

A gardener was working among the flower beds along the river edge of an estate. He looked up to see a blazing steamboat bearing down on him. A moment later the *Henry Clay* struck with terrific force. Her bow slid up the bank twenty-five feet. It had nosed eight feet into the earth of a high railroad embankment. The shock knocked over one of the smokestacks and threw benches and tables about. Many passengers were hurled to decks below or into the water. Pilot Elmendorf, his wife, and the frightened passenger on the bow were thrown to safety on land.

The jolt seemed to have stirred the fires. Flames formed a solid sheet and moved aft. There was no going forward and the stern was over deep water. It was burn or drown, for the passengers who could not swim.

A gentleman seized a large wooden sign—a milliner's advertisement which stood on the deck—and leaped overboard with it. Passengers began to jump into the deep water. A large black boat with a red streak arrived from upriver. It picked up seven people and made for shore, though it could easily have rescued fifteen. A man stood calmly on the upper deck of the *Henry Clay* and threw many wooden chairs

into the water, where drowning passengers grabbed them and floated toward shore.

Mr. Collyer had already reached land. He began breaking up a rail
fence and shoving the pieces out into the water, to people struggling to
stay afloat. Captain Tallman had at last been aroused from his bed. He
was so ill that he could not speak, but he was in the water, helping passenger after passenger to shore. A man threw a wooden settee into the
river and jumped after it. He had just climbed on it when someone
grabbed him by the leg and pulled him off. At that moment he saw his
wife, who could not swim, jump into the water. He worked along the
side of the boat with her to the paddle wheel. They grabbed it, but their
weight caused the wheel to turn and throw them off. Flaming pieces of
wood from the wheel dropped on them. They finally floated to safety on
some of the fence boards.

The gardener, who had first seen the burning boat, and a coach-
man nearby launched a small boat. They saw four men in a sloop who
were robbing the drowning people. The two servants boarded the pirate
sloop and threw the robbers overboard. Then they used the sloop to save
as many as it would hold. One gentleman saved his wife and every one
of his nine children. One at a time they jumped and were towed ashore
by the brave father. Then the whole family carried him away, "entirely
senseless." A train puffed along the bank and stopped. Its men passengers ran down to the river to help in the rescue work.

A Newfoundland dog named Neptune rushed into the water. He
seized a drowning child by her dress and dragged her to safety. He went
back to save a woman, but she was so frightened that the dog had to be
called off.

It was all over in about twenty minutes. Along the shore for over a mile lay hats, shawls, dresses, an occasional body. The *Armenia* drifted in mid-channel. Her two small boats searched the waters for any sign of a living being. But the *Henry Clay* had raced too far ahead of her and they found no one. The train puffed on, carrying a load of the burned and the drowned. Isaac MacDaniel, searching among the bodies on the shore for his dead wife, came upon James Jessup, the clerk who had told him a few hours before that there was no danger.

By five o'clock, nothing was left of the *Henry Clay* except part of the bow. It burned slowly, "like a warning beacon to light up the shapeless wreck of charred timbers and iron below." William Lawrence, coroner of Westchester County, wrote in his tent beside the water that night: "The night was remarkably clear, the full moon dimly lighting up the river and the hills. . . . The surface of the stream was broken only by the oars of a few men who were still dredging for bodies."

The dead were covered that moonlit evening with green boughs. The coroner and his jury had to draw guns and threaten a dark craft filled with men who came to rob. All night long cannon boomed out over the Hudson as the workers ashore tried to dislodge bodies and bring them to the surface of the river.

In the morning, news of the disaster reached New York. The number of dead was reported as eighty. Captain Tallman was already regretting his early statement to a passenger, "There were only ten or fifteen persons drowned and they were common people."

CHAPTER 19

Tin-Horn Rebellion

IN 1844, SLIM DR. SMITH BOUGHTON and his wife moved from Rensselaer County into manor land in Columbia County. A young doctor would not be likely to choose such land on the Hudson. He must have known that in the manors the farmers were poor. He knew the Livingstons and Van Rensselaers would not sell their lands. They just waited for rent payments of hens and wheat and days of labor. When the farmers said the American Revolution had been fought to free men from just such treatment, the manor lords said, "The Livingstons and the Van Rensselaers were heroes of the American Revolution." Then they went on collecting rents from farmers.

The manor lords heard that the young Doctor's calls on his neighbors were not always to help the sick. They heard he was telling the farmers that the landlords did not truly own the lands they claimed. They heard that the Doctor was asking each farmer to pay twenty-five cents a year for each acre he plowed in order to hire lawyers to defend men arrested for not paying their rent.

On a November day, a spy for the manor lords heard a tootle and a boom coming from a near-by field. He tried later to tell his employers what he saw at that moment. To the tune of "Old Dan Tucker," played on a fife and a drum, hundreds of masked men in calico dresses marched around the field. Their masks were of sheepskin, painted red, blue, and yellow. Eyes, noses, and mouths had been painted on them in different colors. The dresses were striped and "made like a woman's nightgown," and they hung below the men's knees. Calico pantaloons showed above farm boots that had been used for plowing. Silken tassels, rattlesnake skins, bright tin horns hung from the belts of the marchers, and jingled as they marched. The men carried weapons in their hands. Each one had a spear or a tomahawk, a pistol or a club, a pitchfork or a rifle.

A big crowd of people cheered the marching men as they stamped around the field and halted before a raised platform. A small figure in a straight-hanging dress stood there, and the calico soldiers raised a shout. "Big Thunder!" they yelled.

The crowd yelled "Big Thunder!" too.

"Down with the rent!" shouted Big Thunder. "The Livingstons and Van Rensselaers have taken from us and our fathers . . . many times what our land is worth. . . . Do not pay them. The Natives you see here (Indians, we call ourselves) will take care of you. . . . the Natives will come out from the rocky glens and caves . . . and drive the rent-collectors off . . ."

Again the men in calico shouted, "Down with the rent!" Someone began to sing and they all joined in. The tune was "Old Dan Tucker,"

but the words were different from those of the old song, for they made
fun of the county's sheriff.

The moon was shining silver bright
The sheriff came at dead of night
High on a hill an Indian true
And on his horn a blast he blew.

Get out of the way, Big Bill Snyder,
We'll tar your coat and feather your hide, sir.

Bill thought he heard the sound of a gun
He cried in fright, O my race is run
Better that I had ne'er been born
Than come within sound of that big horn.

Get out of my way, Big Bill Snyder,
We'll tar your coat and feather your hide, sir.

At moments in the song the singers lifted their tin horns and blew
them. The spy was frightened at the strange proceedings and ran away.

All the upriver towns heard talk that the next big meeting of the
Indians would be at Smoky Hollow on December eighteenth. Big Thunder
had said the Van Rensselaers and the Livingstons did not truly own
their land. The people of Hudson were getting uneasy. The farmers were
saying the Indians would soon gather on the courthouse square in Hudson itself.

The down-renters began arriving at Bam's Tavern in Smoky Hollow early in the cold morning of the eighteenth. Many brought their
dresses and put them on in the upper rooms. Thousands of watchers
made a circle around the silent inn. There was a gunshot and a war

whoop. Then the first masked warrior in calico came out. He leaped and yelled and fired his pistol. All the calico Indians followed him in single file. They blew their horns, and the tails of raccoons and foxes flopped on the backs of their dresses. They shot off their rifles. Suddenly, watchers saw a young man sink to the ground. Blood bubbled from a wound in his chest. A careless parader had shot him through the heart and he was dead. Everybody there knew he was Bill Rifenburg, a boy from a nearby farm. The marching suddenly stopped. Big Thunder spoke. He said that

the shooting of young Rifenburg was a bad mistake. His warriors had brought guns only to protect themselves. They had been afraid they would have to fight off the sheriff, who wanted to arrest them. Then the meeting ended.

Inside the tavern, the calico Indians took off their dresses. A few of them sat by the fireplace and talked. While they were talking, Sheriff Henry Miller walked into the room and said, "Dr. Boughton, you are under arrest." Four men of the Sheriff's posse took Dr. Boughton downstairs.

The Doctor held back. "Help!" he shouted.

There was a thumping fight when the posse tried to pull the prisoner into their carriage. Tin horns were being blown out of the tavern windows. Some of the calico Indians who had started for home were running back.

Then District Attorney Theodore Miller began to speak. He said that no one should stand in the way of the law. It would go hard with anybody who tried to keep the Sheriff from doing his duty. The prisoner would receive a fair trial. While he spoke, the posse forced their prisoner into their carriage. A deputy whipped up the horses and they trotted off.

After the doors of the Hudson jail had closed on the leader of the calico Indians, the town was frightened. The sound of tin horns came from the hills. In the evening, torches moved about on the other side of the river. The men in calico were gathering.

A message came in the morning. It said that if Hudson would not let Dr. Boughton go, a thousand calico Indians would march into the town and burn it down. The mayor ordered the town militia to be ready to fight at the first bell stroke from the Presbyterian Church steeple.

Christmas came.

Hudson children liked that Christmas because an Albany military company in full uniform paraded with drums beating and colors flying, from the railroad station into town. Still, everybody felt that danger was near.

A posse set out on a below-zero morning to capture Walter Hutchins, who was called White Chief by the calico Indians. The posse swooped down on Proper's Tavern south of Hudson, but White Chief had just left. They rode on to Blue Stores, but White Chief was gone. On the next morning, the posse was in Minkville, where White Chief lived. He was not there. They caught sight of him near Gallatin, but he rode into the woods and got away. After a night of shivering at Hot Grounds, the posse came back.

In New York City, Captain Krack's militia troop of German-American cavalry were ordered to move to Hudson at once. They rode their horses on board a steamboat at two o'clock in the morning. Hudson was crowded when they arrived. The troopers had to live on the steamboat that had brought them.

On January third, there was a parade of the troops who had come to protect the town. After the parade, the people of Hudson were no longer afraid. No farmers in calico would dare to attack so large an army, they thought. A military ball was announced for the evening of Wednesday, January eighth, at the big white-pillared hotel, the Hudson House.

The night after this dance, Captain Krack and twenty of his troopers made a sudden sortie on Minkville. There, they captured White Chief, Walter Hutchins. A messenger galloped into Hudson with the news that the mounted troopers would bring their prisoner into the town early in the morning. The townspeople lined the street long before the riders were in sight. Suddenly all talk was hushed by a wild noise. It grew louder, it seemed to be a man's voice. In the midst of the approaching mounted troopers rolled a farm wagon drawn by a team. The crowd saw where the strange noise was coming from. On the floor of the wagon stood Walter Hutchins. He was laughing. He danced about on the wagon boards, pointing at the fancy boots, plumed hats, and shining sabers of Captain Krack's cavalry. He laughed and laughed. All at once the parade of armed men guarding a captive from whom the watchers often bought eggs and butter seemed funny. The squeaking of the wagon and Walter's laughing made the people of Hudson feel ashamed. Tin horns blowing in the night called more for talk than for guns.

A few days later, the embarrassed military companies went home and the citizens of Hudson went back to work. They hoped that the rent troubles were over.

The jury could not agree on a verdict at Dr. Boughton's first trial in March. He was tried again in September. John Van Buren, son of the former president of the nation, Martin Van Buren, was the attorney for the state. White-haired Ambrose L. Jordan was lawyer for the defense.

Judge John W. Edmonds' charge to the jury, after both lawyers had had their say, ended at eight o'clock in the evening. All that night the roads leading to Hudson were choked with wagons, as the farmers rode to town with hope in their hearts. Early the next morning they stood in a great crowd around the courthouse—waiting.

"Guilty," said the foreman of the jury, and Judge Edmonds thanked the jurors. Then he said: "Bring in the prisoner."

The Sheriff marched the prisoner from the jail into the courthouse.

"Have you anything to say why sentence of the law should not be pronounced upon you?"

"I have never done anything forbidden by the country's institutions as I understand them. I beg that my wife be allowed to stay with me in the jail until I am removed."

Then Judge Edmonds said that the crime of which Dr. Boughton was guilty was really high treason—armed rebellion against the lawful government. Until Dr. Boughton had come into the county the farmers had been quiet and orderly. He had come to persuade the farmers to rebel. He had been the first to urge them to wear masks. "Houses have been torn down, farms laid waste, the laws . . . resisted, and the officers of justice fired upon and wounded . . ."

The Judge paused for a moment. Then he said: "The sentence of the Court is that you be confined in the state prison in the county of Clinton at hard labor, for the term of your natural life."

The manor lords had won—against the best leader the farmers had ever had. In the heart of a free land a man still might not own his home without paying unjust rents.

The farmers did not know that in this defeat they had won. They did not know that John Youngs would be swept into the governor's chair at the next year's election. They did not know that John Youngs would pardon Dr. Boughton and many of his loyal friends. They did not know that in 1846, a new state constitution would prevent the manor lords from acting unjustly toward the farmers who had rented their lands. Tenants were set free from all rules the manor lords had demanded they obey. Manor lords and tenants alike would be responsible only to state and national laws.

CHAPTER 20

Ghost Towns
and Ghost Trades

AN ELEVEN-AND-A-HALF FOOT locomotive named the *De Witt Clinton* was taken for a steamboat ride up the Hudson in 1831. It had been built at the West Point Foundry in New York City. It was delivered in Albany at the end of June. On the ninth of August, a group of Albany businessmen rode in three stagecoach cars behind the little engine to Schenectady and back.

Many years were to pass before the people who lived in the houses along the Hudson would know what the coming of the railroads would mean. In 1848, the Hudson River Railroad Company offered the Verplanck family five thousand dollars for the right to run trains over their property. The Verplancks would not listen. Before the end of another year, they were obliged to give over the land to the railroad for only eighteen hundred dollars. Business was going to have its day on the Hudson. Gentle Verplanck was overruled by the rough, tough owners of the railroad.

Nathaniel Parker Willis, a curly-haired, pink-cheeked poet, spent much time along the Hudson. Sometimes he rode the mare, Lady Jane, while his smooth-haired terrier, Flippertigibbet, nipped at her heels. Sometimes he rode Black Prince, while Don, his black Newfoundland dog, bounded along behind. Often he wrote about what he discovered on these rides. He wrote that farmers were selling the river front lands they had bought earlier in the century for two hundred dollars an acre to the new-rich princes of American business. These men could pay well for scenery. Some of them bought lands out of sight of the water for five dollars an acre. Willis saw lanky mountain men bringing to the river landings wagonloads of "mountain wheat"—young hickory saplings— to be sold for hop poles. He watched men loading freight steamers with fruit and vegetables grown on west bank. He saw them leave the Cornwall docks at nine o'clock in the evening for New York City, and he knew they would arrive at three in the morning. He knew that the new traders along the river valley were making money. He saw the homes of the newly rich rising among blooming gardens.

Mr. Willis also noted that one early river-shore business was not

pleasing to the owners of estates. To them, it was unsightly and it brought crowds of immigrants. A Tarrytown Dutchman named Van Loon had found that he could dry clays, add sand, and bake the mixture into bricks. The number of brickyards at the water's edge grew large. They gave a hearty welcome to thousands of Irishmen who came to America looking for work.

When the Irish were the "brickyarders," making bricks was a longer and harder job than it is now. Today, the brickmaking industry continues to flourish in the Hudson valley. But barges loaded with bricks still go down the Hudson as they did a hundred years ago.

Brickmaking was not the only growing business in the Hudson valley that looked to Irish workers for help. Their axes cut down hemlocks to be stripped of their bark for the valley tanneries. In the region where the German tarmakers had cut pitch pines in 1710, Yankee barkpeelers began to tan leather over a hundred years later. But it was not until after the Irish had come that tanning reached its peak. Then freighters came up the river. Their crews sang Spanish songs to the music of guitars. They unloaded thousands of salt-rubbed cowhides from Argentina and Brazil upon the docks of river towns.

Teamsters drove wagons loaded with sole leather for shoes along the roads of the steep Highlands. They urged their horses to drag loads of raw South American hides from the docks up to the tanneries. Quilted clouds of yellow smoke hung above each busy tannery.

Gradually, the hemlocks disappeared from the woods and tanning on the Hudson was forced to an end. Only the old walls of the tanneries tell the story now.

In the winter months, the Hudson gave many men work as soon as cold weather froze it. When the ice had reached a thickness of ten inches, the stream's cold, dry surface would be quickly streaked with dark man-made canals. Thousands of men would be working beside these. All day and all night they would cut ice furiously, afraid that a drop in temperature would make it too thick or a thaw would make it too thin. The cutters sawed large ice cakes from the edges of the canals and pushed them into open water. Other workers poled the pieces toward shore. There, they were tumbled in pairs on moving belts that carried them upward into big storehouses. Covered with sawdust, the ice was stored until summer when it would be loaded on scows bound for hot New York City. Even the servants in the big houses hurried to dry the supper dishes in order to join the ice cutters. They could earn a little extra during the winter evenings, while torches flared and the canals were alive with bobbing ice cakes. Now that ice is made in modern refrigerators, farmers have been growing mushrooms in the old storehouses.

But of all the Hudson's booming mid-nineteenth century trades, none brought such wild days as the cement works. The builders of the hundred-mile Delaware & Hudson Canal began work in 1825. Hundreds of Yankee, Dutch, and Irish workers came to the country south of Kingston to dig it. The diggers uncovered below ground a cement which, though slow to set, was very hard. Suddenly, the mountain town of Rosendale near the mines began to grow. In a few weeks, it was like the mining towns of the Far West. It became a town of three thousand hard-drinking, hard-fighting "cement burners." At the end of a day, they poured out of the mountain cement mines and charged down into the town. After long hours of digging in dark caves, the workers plunged into a night of wild doings.

There was a famous night when Irish Jack Dillon met on the Rosendale Bridge a gang of his own countrymen from downriver.

"Anything on your mind?" said one of them.

"Not a thing," said Jack, and hit him between the eyes.

The width of the bridge allowed only two men to reach Jack at a time, so he used his left hand to lick one of them while his right beat down the other. It took Jack most of the night, because all the Irish in town heard about the fight and lined up in two columns to wait their turn. By morning, Jack had beaten the whole lot of them.

There is Rosendale cement in Brooklyn Bridge, in the base of the Statue of Liberty, and in Croton Aqueduct that once piped fresh water from Croton Reservoir all the way to New York City. The cement lasts almost as well as the stones it binds together. The workers dug a lot of it out of the west-bank hills by the Hudson, and left behind cold, damp caves. Some Ulster County people say you can walk all the way from Rosendale to Kingston through the middle of the earth, if you know the way. Others say it is so cold in one of the caverns that the underground lake which has formed there stays frozen the year round, and mid-summer skating parties could be held if the guests could find their way to it.

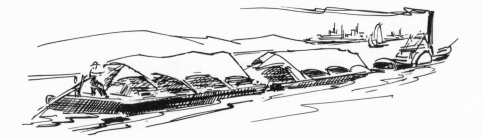

CHAPTER 21

They Loved
the Mary Powell

T HE HUDSON VALLEY LOVED THE *Mary Powell.* People who are more than sixty years old still love her. Her slim white image moves, swift and quiet, in their memories. "She was a lovely boat," they say. "Her bell had a silver tongue. Her whistle was a golden sound."

Captain Absalom Anderson planned her in 1861, and she was built by Michael Allison in Jersey City. From the hour she came into the Hudson, she was the river queen.

In vain, the other captains tried to take her trade away. The *Armenia* tooted proudly on her new thirty-four-whistle calliope, raising echoes with "The Belle of the Mohawk Vale" and "Jordan's a Hard Road to Travel." The *Glen Cove* and the *General Sedgwick* blew steam through the pipes of their whistle organs, but the people loved the *Mary Powell* most of all.

But no tricks of the rival captains made a difference to the *Mary Powell*. She skimmed past the swiftest, not stirring a ripple on a cup of coffee in her dining room. Some people used to say Captain Anderson hired a Negro boy just to keep the flies from lighting on her rail and slowing her with their weight. They claimed he mixed whale's grease into her paint to give her easy sliding through the water. And once an unknown poet said, "He hitched her to a porpoise four-in-hand."

She steamed away from Kingston in the morning. She moored below New York City's high towers at noon. At three, she began to move upriver. At nine, her silver bell was sounding over the dark waters of Rondout Creek. Then, the sweet voice of deckhand Seymour Darling was calling, as it called for thirty-four years, "Last stop, home port, Kingston Landing!" Captain Anderson ran a family boat and everyone could feel safe on her. Even small children were often put in his care to make a trip without their fathers and mothers.

The *Mary Powell* never had a bad accident. She never lost a passenger. She carried fathers from hot labor in the city to cool riverside homes where their families waited. She was a honeymoon boat; she was a children's boat. She carried young boys to West Point, and she brought them back officers in the United States Army. She once brought a coffin wrapped in a flag to West Point. Inside it lay the body of General George Custer. The Indians of the Western plains had won his yellow hair.

The river families still say, "you could depend upon the *Mary Powell*. She was always on time." They laugh and say the Military Academy used to time its drills by the sound of her bell. Even on the day a cyclone tumbled her stacks overboard, pilot Guernsey Betts brought her into Rondout on time. On ordinary days, she had minutes to spare.

The *Mary Powell* never wasted effort at a landing. Sometimes

Guernsey Betts did not bother to make fast her landing lines. He just held her up against the dock while the gangplank was run ashore and the passengers came aboard. Then he would give the boys in the engine room a jingle and she would be off like a race horse. She could slip into top speed while other boats were slowly leaving their docks. Betts used to say the only time she ever gave him trouble was when he would try to pass the mouth of Rondout Creek on a trip to Albany. She was so used to turning in there that she would bear to the left no matter how firmly he held the wheel.

When Absalom Anderson died, his son, A. E. Anderson became the captain of the *Mary Powell*. She grew old gracefully, and he grew old with her. Before her nearly sixty years were over, she was known and loved not only in America, but in all countries of the world. Captain Anderson II died before she made her last journey. She ended her career faithfully, on the Day Line run.

The junk dealer, John Fisher, dismantled the *Mary Powell* at Sunflower Dock on Rondout Creek. Her silver bell came down from above the wheelhouse, and was given to the New York Historical Society by Alfred Van Santvoord Olcott, a former president of the Hudson River Day Line. The packet, *Robert Fulton,* now speaks with the deep voice of her whistle. The pilot wheel that Guernsey Betts's hands knew so well stands in the Senate House Museum at Kingston.

But the *Mary Powell* lives in more than the relics of her past. She is a lovely image in thousands of memories. "She had a silver tongue," people say. "She had a golden throat."

CHAPTER 22

Flow On

For NEARLY THREE HUNDRED YEARS, the people in the Hudson valley tried to own land along the river—and failed. The manor lords would not let them buy their farms. The new-rich kept their less rich countrymen off the shore until about 1900. Then, slowly and in an unexpected way, the people began to win the river lands.

Just before the twentieth century began, Newport, Rhode Island, and other fashionable centers drew the owners of great estates away from the Hudson. Big homes were closed. Real-estate prices dropped. The old estates offered many advantages to tax-free organizations seeking sites for schools and religious groups.

Today, some stretches of the stream seem to be wholly occupied by schools, churches, and retreats. Out of eighty elaborate houses, each bearing a name such as "Rose Hill," "Placentia," "Mount Gulian," a historian recently found that thirty-three were no longer operated as private estates.

Thus, in a strange way, the people have won the river. It is not the way they had planned. They had dreamed a man might own his own plot beside the water. There he might tie his boat outside the front door. He might fish from his own pier. He might swim from his own beach. He might grow his crops on land beside the water.

The people are finding other ways of owning the river today. Some of them are old ways, which they have found once more. The shad are running as they used to, and the men in the low, weathered shacks be-

side the water catch and sell them. Some of the old river businesses—
the mining of cement and the making of bricks—have been revived.
The trim ships of the Hudson River Day Line still carry their millions
of passengers on happy excursions every season. The big *Alexander
Hamilton* looks cool and uncrowded even when she has five thousand
passengers aboard, as she often does. She and the *Peter Stuyvesant* of
the Day Line carry thousands of children up the river to Catskill camps
at the beginning of every summer. Nearly all of them come back on the
Alexander Hamilton shortly before Labor Day. Then, the big steamer
delivers about three thousand singing, dancing, sun-tanned children to
parents waiting on the New York docks.

Vessels other than those of the beloved Day Line are trafficking on
the river. Nearly every summer day the riverboats whistle salutes to sea-
going ships bound for Albany. They carry cargoes from Buenos Aires,
Rosario, LaPlata in the Argentine, from Yokohama and Osaka in Japan,
from Surabaya in Java and Viipuri in Finland, from Bombay in India,
and Hudiksvall and Härnösand in Sweden, from Leningrad in Russia,
and from Bergen in Norway. From Albany, on their long journeys home,
they take Hudson valley corn and lumber, and the things men who
work beside the river make—automobiles, business machines, auto-
matic heaters, copper wire, and hundreds of other products.

South of Albany, along the river, lies a fruit belt where farmers
grow apples and sell them. Others grow acres of grapes that are made
into wine. North of Albany, the melon fields lie along the stream. People
who live there say Hudson valley melons taste better than other melons.
Growers send truckloads and boatloads of them down the river.

The valley people have loved the big stream long, and they have
shown their love. They dreamed once of a river lined with little farms.

They are working now to make another and different dream come true.

The Hudson of the people's present dream is a river of clean waters. They want their children to swim in it as safely as did the Algonkin boys and girls before the days of the white explorers.

The people of the big valley know that freeing the Hudson water of pollution from factory waste, from sewage, and dumped impurities will take time; but they know, too, that it will be done. They know what cleansed and purified waters could do for them and their children. There will be beaches on the Hudson. The people will sit in the sun. They will swim in the water.

There will be boating for everybody, the people say. Up and down the banks, where the water is deep enough for boating, there will be basins or marinas. In a marina, a man can moor his canoe or his rowboat or his yacht. He can buy supplies there, too. He can take his family on journeys from a marina base along Henry Hudson's "Great River of the Mountains."

A good time will come soon. Then the river will ripple beside green parks and winding level roads all of its way to the tall gray city at its mouth. Its banks will not be scarred by rock quarries, but will be covered with new greenery. They will not be made ugly with advertising signboards. Soon the whole course of the stream will be beautiful. Big business corporations along the Hudson are working with the people who live there to make the valley beautiful. Their factories, experimental laboratories, and offices are set in acres as pleasant and attractive as those of the old well-cared-for estates.

Many organizations are working in the interest of the citizens of the valley. The Hudson River Conservation Society is constantly ready to defend the great stream from any influences that may destroy its quality. The Palisades Interstate Park Commission has created an area of woods and fields and streams that offer all the people of the region rest and recreation. The American Scenic and Historic Preservation Society and other patriotic groups devoted to the restoring of the buildings of our noble past—historic buildings at West Point, Sleepy Hollow, Boscobel, Ticonderoga and Saratoga—are preserving the exciting reminders of our nation's history in the valley, and are creating a fitting home for a happy people beside a free and mighty river.

About the Author

CARL CARMER, editor of the famous "Rivers of America" series, is also the author of *The Hudson* and numerous other best-selling books. His position in the literary world is an outstanding one. Among his honors has been the New York *Herald Tribune* Children's Spring Book Festival Award. He has been president of P.E.N. and the Poetry Society of America, is honorary vice-president of the New York Folklore Society, and is a Councillor of the Society of American Historians.

After receiving a B.A. from Hamilton College and an M.A. from Harvard, Mr. Carmer taught for twelve years at Syracuse University, the University of Rochester, Hamilton College, and the University of Alabama. He then became a columnist for the New Orleans *Morning Tribune*. Later, in New York, he was an editor for *Vanity Fair* and *Theatre Arts Monthly*.

Since the publication of his best-selling book, *Stars Fell on Alabama*, in 1934, Mr. Carmer has devoted most of his time to writing. He now lives in century-old Octagon House on the banks of the Hudson River.

4